THE WEIRD WORLD ROLLS ON

A Collection of Poems

Jean Davies Okimoto

EDITOR

ENDICOTT AND HUGH BOOKS

Proceeds from the sale of this book are donated to Vashon Community Care

Copyright © 2012, Endicott and Hugh Books

All rights reserved. No part of this work may be used or reproduced in any manner whatsoever without written permission from the contributors, except in the case of brief quotations embodied in critical articles are reviews. Contributors may be reached in care of Endicott and Hugh Books: info@endicottandhughbooks.com

The Weird World Rolls On: A Collection of Poems

ISBN: 978-0-9837115-6-8

"Violets for Mother," "Beasts from the Heart," "Her Words to No One: 1946," Lonny Kaneko, published in *Coming Home From Camp*, Brooding Heron Press, *1986*
"Carnival," Lynda Schraufnagel, published in *Feminist Studies*, Vol. 13, 1987

Cover design: Masha Shubin
Back cover photograph/design: ©Roger Davies

Printed in the United States

Endicott and Hugh Books
P.O. Box 13305
Burton, WA 98013
www.endicottandhughbooks.com

FOREWORD

In 1968 during the Vietnam war, my brother Roger Davies found a home in Canada. He became a Canadian citizen and has been a teacher in Ontario, Newfoundland and Nova Scotia. A Quaker and a peace activist, he is also a poet and for years has been sending poems to me in emails, and for years I've wanted to see them published. My brother visited Vashon Island where our mother, Edie Davies, spent the last months of her life at Vashon Community Care. Vashon Island is home to many people in the arts, among them quite a few poets.

One of the whimsical island treasures is the Hiway Haiku. Near the north end ferry dock are three Burma Shave type signs, with one line of a haiku written in beautiful calligraphy on each sign. This charming project was founded by Hita vonMende and Kajira Wyn Berry. Kaj is a calligrapher and a member of Mondays at Three, a haiku writing group which supplies many of haikus for Hiway Haikus. Like most islanders and visitors to Vashon, I love the haikus and thought they'd make a good addition to this collection. And then it wasn't long before I realized that I knew, and with the help of poets Jill Andrews and Ann Spiers—knew of, quite a few other poets and I wanted to include their work as well.

Some of the poets in this collection have been published in various journals and anthologies—or published chapbooks, and others are just beginning to write poetry. When I was trying to find a title that would encompass the diversity of the subjects in the collection, I stumbled across a line from a poem that Nina Sankovitch refers to in her memoir of reading, *Tolstoy and the Purple Chair*. The line, "the weird world rolls on" comes from a poem written in the late 1800's by Rose Hawthorne Lathrop, the daughter of Nathaniel Hawthorne.

In describing her work, the great poet Adrienne Rich said, "I think my work comes out of both an intense desire for connection and what it means to feel isolated. There's always going to be a kind of tidal movement back and forth between the two. Art and literature have given so many people the relief of feeling connected—pulled us out of isolation. It has let us know that somebody else breathed and dreamed and had sex and loved and raged and knew loneliness the way we do." And as the Irish poet Brendan Kennelly put it, "poetry is one of the most vital treasures that humanity possesses; it is a bridge between separated souls." To add to this bridge we are pleased to offer this collection.

Jeanie Okimoto
Editor
Vashon Island, May 2012

CONTENTS

JEAN AMELUXEN
  Haiku 5, 30, 94, 163

JILL BRADENFELS ANDREWS
  Afflicted 130
  Haiku 28, 31, 75, 86, 118
  Skagit Swing 47
  Your Odyssey 107

PAUL BACKSTROM
  Clam Viewing Sculpture at 4th and Madison 10
  Landmarks 81

DOROTHY HALL BAUER
  He Remembered, I Forgot 35

KAJIRA WYN BERRY
  Haiku 9, 13, 25, 97

JEAN CARPENTER
  Divorce Mississippi Style 40
  I Met April Today 173
  My Best Things 110

MARTA COU
  Cuba of My Heart 184
  Haiku 171
  Longing 106
  Nostalgia Habanera 89

ROGER DAVIES
  Earth Hour 191
  Facebook Poem 181
  Fifties 199
  Haiku 69, 83, 209
  Information 150
  In Praise of the Pretend and the Rumpled 165

 Kindle 4
 Leaf Bud Futures 144
 Michigan January 95
 Nostalgia 88
 On The Occasion of the Bombing of Yugoslavia 166
 Poem Juice 1
 Prayer in the Form of Cranes 205
 Preparing to Pretend to Knit at the Chemotherapy Clinic 175
 Running Wild 36
 Sentence Love 16
 Small Poem I 6
 Summer 18
 Tenses 17
 The Argentinean Blueberries 183
 The Matters-at-Hand 103
 The Surface 91
 Unclear Cut 141
 What to Do With Political Ideas 139
 When I'm Seventy 70
 Wishful Thinking 167

C. HUNTER DAVIS
 A Cottonwood on My Birthday 156
 Apples Fall 192
 Calling for Lillie 164
 Christmas Eve Dinner 155
 Communities 142
 Embrace 143
 Going 131
 Sea Lions on the Warning Buoy 66
 The Bus Stop 177
 The Lake Swimmers 37

MICHAEL FEINSTEIN
 Haiku 24, 68, 82, 87, 99, 212
 Thirteen Ways 26

SHIRLEY FERRIS
 Haiku 12, 39, 62, 90, 172

MARGARET HELDRING
 Schoolhouse on Vashon 113

AUGUST (GUS) HOLMES
Untitled 213

ERIC HORSTING
1945: Oma In Amsterdam As The War Ends 197
Coal Miners and Other People.. 188
Damaged Goods 109
Heroism 176
Holland: Hongerwinter, 1944-45 (The War Years End) 194
Manifesto 198
Mortality 186
Opening Nights 84
Spring 170
Writing Again, In Maine 2

CATHERINE JOHNSON
For Jacinta 123
May Swim off the Coast of Clare 77
On a Bright Summer Day 182
Waking 105

KATE JOHNSON
Septima.. 111

LONNY KANEKO
Agoraphobia 1955... 55
Beasts From the Heart 132
Body of Evidence... 49
Clothes Make the Man 73
Coming Home from Camp
   Her words to no one:1946 195
Falling Man 43
Pre-Speech 65
Purple Heart.. 57
Rushing through the Gravel at 99 60
Sadness Is Not a River 34
Violets for Mother... 61

CAL KINNEAR
An Other Eye... 138
A Peony 179
By a Road I Don't Usually Take 29
Dreamtime... 180
Klompen Clogs 98

My Map 15
　　Of Hands 45
　　Outside 52
　　(The Names) 140
　　Turning Color 145

JULI GOETZ MORSER
　　Gifts 48
　　Harts Pass 21
　　March 14 115
　　Pastels 122
　　Poem from Afar 50
　　The Timeless Shuffle 46
　　What if We Knew 168
　　What Morning Brings 104

EDEEN MARLOWE PARISH
　　An April Day 120

JANICE RANDALL
　　Crooked Road 51
　　Descent 53
　　Home 189
　　North Beach Sunday 85
　　Roses in the Snow 119
　　Solace 22
　　The Laundress 136

HELEN RUSSELL
　　Haiku 71, 135, 161, 210, 211

LYNDA SCHRAUFNAGEL
　　Carnival 63
　　Comfort 162
　　On Broadway 42

MARY G. L. SHACKELFORD
　　Fall Poem - October 11, 2001 202
　　February Prunings 2011 58
　　Full Moon in April 100
　　Halfway to Spring Equinox 101
　　New Year 67
　　Surfeit 169
　　Uncovered Ground 126

RON SIMONS
- Haiku 23, 32, 134, 159

ANN SPIERS
- Elegy for Bill 19
- Haiku 92, 96, 114, 129
- Kitchen Help 74
- Lavender Harvest 152
- Mushroom 160

INA WHITLOCK
- 60 Seconds 207
- Blackberry Time 11
- Blue Glass 125
- Christmas 2010 146
- Clam Shells 8
- Croak On 208
- Farewell 33
- High Tide 190
- Moon Over Snow 93
- Old Pants, Old Shirt 72
- Quartet on a Theme of Shostakovich 200
- Thumb Power 151
- Too Much 149
- Travel 108
- Unless 201
- Will the Time Come? 187

SUSAN GRAY WILEY
- Angel Wings 76
- A Run 117
- Cheli La Pass - Bhutan 78
- Mt. Rainier 79
- Rebuilding 20
- Remembering Watermelon 14
- Thanksgiving Cactus 154
- Through the Looking Glass 193
- Turn It Down 148
- Wrapped Up 128

CONTRIBUTORS   215

ROGER DAVIES

Poem Juice

I am going to the corner store now
to pick up a bottle of poem, maybe
two litres this time: Enough to pour
into my car then it will flap like a goose
flapping out of the library parking lot,
and some to send to the politicians
sitting on their hands and being peckish
a slug of poem will set them straight,
singing lullabies and wearing fedoras
and feathers. In the old days we said
we'd put LSD in the water and teach
LBJ and his bro's a lesson or two, but
now it is 07 we have something organic
for grownups in the form of jus de poem.
Put some in the Taliban's tea.
Divvy some out into the endless plastic
wine glasses lined up like soldiers
on the white parade grounds.
Give some to the kids
but no more than they can handle.
Close the blinds and invite your friends over.
Sell it on the street like lemonade,
keeping the aged stuff for yourself.

ERIC HORSTING

Writing Again, In Maine

After months of silence, the solitary pines
bless me with those voices I haven't heard;
it seems too easy, this mindless surge of lines,
this simple setting out of word, word, word,

but I let it be: notice
the orange fox
in the meadow, see how the sheep lie down
together, the Jersey flicks the flies and walks
about the hilly pasture and around

the pump gate, waiting for the evening rain
to wet the grass. None of this finds a place
in my story, which wanders on again,
where it will, with never a pause to erase

false starts. There are none. The Jersey lies down
near the fence and sleeps. The sheep waddle off
like sheep. My hand, its pen, abates, slows down,
and you, who sense this, signal, with your cough,

it's time for us to meander, to work
out the stiffness in the spine and thumb
that comes from sitting all these hours, that lurks
beneath the language that's kept us dumb

since noon. An hour later, we stop along
the gravel road, pick raspberries, a few.
For the first time, I don't bite, just press. The song
of their juice drowns my tongue. I look at you.

The pits slide, silent, whole, down my throat,
tiny placebos. My body slouches. I see
how strong ease is, and I can concentrate,
once more, on how we like each other, let be.

ROGER DAVIES

Kindle

I'm not having much luck
rubbing two sticks together

so I reach into the bag
at my waist

the companion bag
I've had since childhood

in which I've stashed
my collection of found words

some tarnished and worn and treasured
some bright and shiny and untested

some like coins with their familiar faces
some I can only guess at —

I pull out *silk* and *skin*...

with which I get first smoke
then the hopeful sign of blue glow

rubbing them together
striving to get some mind focus

like a magnifier in sunlight
I hope for heat in this damp surround

JEAN AMELUXEN

Winters' old poems
written in the cursive script
of long frozen grass

ROGER DAVIES

Small Poem I

Death & Destruction
big before us
pushes our buttons:
atomic bombs,
super Nova,
black holes,
even the flattening
of an old hotel.

It's easy
to discount
the sub-atomic
losses, and
the myriad
of bugs
going to oblivion
each first frost.

Remember, then,
the courageous
members of
The Small Losses Orchestra
tuning to the out-going
breath, the closing
of the corner store,
the friendship
knocked down
a notch, the beloved dog
leaping less.

No need
for bunker busters
and the attendant
gov't issue
lies—

When our
personal headlines
speak the small
truths of our
precious, numbered
days

INA WHITLOCK

Clam Shells

Northwestern tide crochets
   a shawl in watery glaze
      of limpets, pebbles, sands
         beyond numbering,
  awash
in watery songs, and arias
      of life and love and
  death–
    two clam shells, one
   clasped high,
  the other at her waist,
Carmen dances with castanets.

KAJIRA WYN BERRY

Summer is over
and we part, like eyelids,
like clams opening

PAUL BACKSTROM

Clam Viewing Sculpture at 4th and Madison

No Lumbago
    Lordosis
        Laminectomy
My acre's happy two tides a day.
Still, sometimes, I leave the bed
And soar like Superman In my invertebrate dreams.

INA WHITLOCK

Blackberry Time

    Here, again,
    where memory is gain of years
    and blackberries pace a season
    of indulgence and work, picking
    the ripe from an untimely pluck
    by a soft squeeze of the dark
    sweet globules, savoring,
    in wisdom and luck, the recall
    and endeavor, of not stretching too far
    or balance be lost to thorns,
    torturous vines, scratched veins,
    blackberry stains, caught –
Caught again!

SHIRLEY FERRIS

Snooze in the hammock
reverie interrupted
by a single bee

KAJIRA WYN BERRY

deep enough to drown in
this high summer day
the young sky, so blue

SUSAN GRAY WILEY

Remembering Watermelon

Thumped, bumped, sniffed
Knife penetrates splitting skin
Sounds crack the break
Opening heart to waiting vigil faces.

Equal divisions squirt out
    puddle, reflect
        hands grab
For a piece of fruit, day, or life.

It matters if seeds hit their targets
If vines grow through deck boards.

The cutting to past goes deep
    collected as pink tonic
dripped from luscious summer lips.

My Map

It's time everything came indoors.
No more large spaces, only those
that can be folded into the pages of an Atlas.
A bear on the basement stairs,
an owl in the attic window.
It's time to deal with what's nearest at hand,
what's too close to think about.

ROGER DAVIES

Sentence Love

....the crispness of your beginnings, and endings....
....you let me know how to get started with you....

I'm drawn to the welcoming flag of your big first letter,
and to the place of your space before, so restful
before journeying along with the words.

Sometimes you are short, brief, terse,
like a cold bracing wind in my raised face.

Other times, a warm summer stream,
flowing and meandering, with ripples and runs
and quiet pools sheltered by the perfect punctuation
for just such a moment.
How gentle and reassuring! And thank you beloved Sentence
for taking my hand and guiding me with
your little helpful marks—commas, dashes,
and dots.

I've known you to open the curtain
with a ta-da!, and I've known you, too,
to give me a subtle partial peek,
me raising slowly one eyelid.

I like your warm presence
with sadnesses,
before me on the page
as if punctuated by a single tear
dropping to the cheek
as a period, or question mark.

ROGER DAVIES

Tenses

My ESL student, a refugee from Nepal,
asks about the past, present, and future
tenses. I draw a line with pleasantly
pointy arrows at both ends, signaling
that time seemingly goes on forever
in both directions. Let's say this dot
is now. I put the dot here; I am
putting the dot here. Sometime,
somewhere in the past events
began, went on for awhile, then
ended. How do we talk about them?
Or want to forget or keep to ourselves,
I think to myself. In a few minutes
into the future, I can imagine
myself getting out my scissors,
cutting out the timeline and forming
a circle, Kumar looking on quizzically,
knowingly. We will be placing
our circle between the 900 stacks,
where we can always make room
for ourselves, then tossing our
bright, featherweight, now near
worthless pennies toward the ring,
smiling at both hits and misses.

ROGER DAVIES

Summer

summer people
hoky-pokying
through

life, then

put your
whole body in

forever

and that's what it's all about

ANN SPIERS

Elegy for Bill

They took the dogs away today.
Noon, deer enter the garden
    to eat the best roses.

In the workyard,
    I sort out his tools and paint,
    good stuff for the garage sale.

I leave nails and lids.
Crows will pick through these.
    So much forgotten.

I open the house to give it air
    before the nieces come,
    years gone, chatting, long faces.

I sit at his table,
    slather apple butter
    on the husky bread.

Stellers jay at the window
    —rat ta tat tat tattat—
    begging its daily bread.

The nieces are bothered
    by everything, and I by them.
At the window again

the jay: rat ta tat tat tattat.
I open the window
    to tell it Bill is dead.

SUSAN GRAY WILEY

Rebuilding

"It was a blessing" most say,
A way to trash yellowed stained photos
and greased up jokes left hanging
by unnecessary nails
in my Father's drowned cabin.

"A blessing in disguise"
no more clam steamed walls
papered pot-belly black
from bellowed flames and swearing
or clocks measuring tides and drinking.

Gone are peeling deck boards
from spitting seeds
and splintered baby toes

Gone are hills weaving sky
around heron calls
A place to test gulls
with overhand bread throws

Geometric glass now shape the view
Sheet Rock and Metal separate
Polygons define hills
outline water
hold a sky.

I try to feel warmth in push button fire
but instead crawl wet sand, clawing clues
scratching out old rocks
desperate to find
the Lifeline.

JULI GOETZ MORSER

Harts Pass

Still point in the sleepless night
Coyotes corral
Yips pierce the present darkness
Whispers of insomnia drift down the hall.

When death happens
All dissolves
The restless, the relentless chatter
Demanding, dictating sense be had of our daily lives.

Brilliant pricks of light
Like the stars we are
But moments in a late August night
Gone when dawn unfurls.

If this is but illusion
What stunning swales of evergreen spears
What elegant shadows thrown on chartreuse alpine grasses
I see
Along the dust crunched trail of Hart's Pass
Contrasted with the scorched, aching emptiness
Believed in the mid of night,
A picture of bleakness

Softened in turn
By the murmur of friends rising below,
Coffee's brewed scent slipping up the staircase
To wake me from slumber.

There is nothing but this
And then it is gone.

JANICE RANDALL

Solace

Daily baptismal ritual chlorine dips
Wash daily sins downspout drains
Warm watery blessings shower rivulets across bare backs
Blasting hot jets melt stress into smooth sacred moments
Aquamarine bubbles leave troubled days past
      Respite in the land of rain and wind.

Few seek solace in luminous night waters
Meditate on ripples splashing wet against turquoise tiles
Undulating movement lifts weightless bodies
Rhythmic strokes blue cement echoes
Keep time with bobbing goggled heads
      Lost in the land of sideways rain and fierce wind.

120 degrees and rising
Heat seeps deep between sinewy muscle fibers
Steel nail heads singe soft, slick flesh
Inflicts innocent pain in dim cedar sanctuary
Silence smells sweeter than incense
      Solace found soaking in this land of relentless rain and wind.

RON SIMONS

Too far back in line
To get onto this ferry
Rain. A newspaper

MICHAEL FEINSTEIN

stillness of sunrise
on flat seas, my dog and I
choose not to talk much

KAJIRA WYN BERRY

mailboxes appear
like dreams of soldiers marching
—early morning fog

MICHAEL FEINSTEIN

Thirteen Ways
With apologies to Wallace Stevens

I.
Among ten thousand snowy mountains,
the only moving thing
was the vine of the blackberry.

II.
I was of three minds,
the blackberry—runners
creeping—of one.

III.
Behind the house for sale,
blackberries on the move.

IV.
Trail's edge, blackberry
vines closing in.
What is a path
but someone's dream?

V.
O capped men of Enumclaw,
do you feel the mountain
rumbling in your boots?
Can you hear the
blackberries growing?

VI.
Today, the first blackberry
sweet on my tongue,
my father gone now
forty-two years.

VII.
Clusters in a dark galaxy,
crushed, each succulent globe
an explosion of sunlight.

VIII.
Clouds after sun, the smell of rain,
blackberry leaves turning up in the wind.

IX.
Late summer, Sunday,
blackberries, vine-spent,
fading to gray.

X.
Loneliness of beach shells,
the sea's emptiness
after the loon dives,
blackberry dreams
dried and brittle.

XI.
This morning, a scent
of woodsmoke in the blackberries,
somewhere a stove door closes.

XII.
Sky moving north,
blackberries puckering, winter
on the mind's edge.

XIII.
It was evening all afternoon.
It was raining
and it was going to rain.
Raven perched
in the blackberry canes.

JILL BRADENFELS ANDREWS

> Sky full of swallows
> handfull of weeds
> gardening at dusk

CAL KINNEAR

By a Road I Don't Usually Take

By a road I don't usually take,
heading home: off to the right there,
beside a mobile home,
about 40 feet long, white-
hulled, bluff-bowed,
a sturdy cabin,
maybe a small ferry from
a century ago.
Clear up here dry-
docked at the top of the island. Like
anchoring down a cumulus rack
in the back yard by the wood pile,
or a strayed angel
in a chicken coop.
Something out of the farthest reaches
of the Cauca, the Magdalena, the Orinoco,
the Amazon.
Full of pulse and surge, not
to be cribbed down
in long grass.

JEAN AMELUXEN

Outside a vacant house
chimes play a tune
that only the wind will hear

JILL BRADENFELS ANDREWS

atop the pine
a white crowned sparrow
sings down the sun.

RON SIMONS

Inching up to the stoplight
Arranging the moon
Among the branches

INA WHITLOCK

Farewell

Sadness lingers under canopy
of Ironwood's brittle shroud;
first light, through scraggly limbs
filters a scrunch of needles underfoot
where I search for you, the missing one.

Ironwood's island underworld
where night violence of machete split
the hoary husk of coconut's sweet flesh–
a Cardinal sips, sucks, tweets, a bacchanal
of Glorias in gelatinous mess.

Dawn brushes the earth red.
Sun paints in plaintive splendor
grief's distraught fire with exuberant light,
lifts death from Ironwood's shelter.
Cardinal sings the earth alive, again.

LONNY KANEKO

Sadness Is Not a River

Sadness is not a river that flows through the daily plain;
It is a flood that has overflowed its banks and reaches
Around every rock and deep into the roots of ferns
And Douglas fir, into crevices left by army ants and bees,
Where it sits soaking into the horizon waiting for a flame
To ignite the quiet depression that is drowning its victim
In the oil and kerosene of private immolation. Where is Joy,
The beautiful long legged demon of youth that draws
The eyes of men and women alike? Where is June,
That winged creature that soars through clouds, her fiery eyes
Ablaze with the spirit of sunrise? Gone, for Time is the river
That overflows its aging banks, overwhelmed by the rush
That accumulates from months of snows. When day reopens
Its morning window, my mother rises Like the winter sun,
Struggling through the foggy thoughts and ailing vision
That blurs light and darkness into ordinary gray.
Although summer light has faded, the pain
Of rising and falling must sustain each day.

DOROTHY HALL BAUER

He Remembered, I Forgot

He remembered. I forgot
I had no brain injury
No long coma
I wasn't that passenger
I wasn't the one in the ditch
The one twitching in the hospital bed.

I was traveling to far countries
I saw the golden dome of Jerusalem
The wild birds of Eilat
I forgot our pact
"We'll meet at the bus stop."

The man looked familiar. That
baseball hat, that nose
Yes, yes, it's Robin
"Hi" I said. I smiled, glad to see him.
Then I saw his face
Anger, disbelief, irritation, sorrow
He knew. He knew I forgot.

There was that other time
"It's time for me to pick up my son"
"He'll be alright. They all get together there."
I can't forget that little boy still there, still waiting
In the dark.

But Robin is forgiving
When I came back from Africa
There he was
"I called the airport to find out if you were on this flight" He said.
    He was there
Ready to help me
Carry my luggage.

ROGER DAVIES

Running Wild

When the old man
saw a waterfall on TV,
in an ad for Cuban vacations

he called his travel agent
right away
booking the next flight
for Cuba. When his son
got word

a call went in
to the agent
saying my father
has Alzheimer's,
he's been trying to live out
his life in poems; it's his
imagination running,
wild.

C. HUNTER DAVIS

The Lake Swimmers

It is their custom to swim
when morning soup steams
through the lake.
As many as 9 have come
webbed in neoprene
they lap parallel to the shore.

You would watch from the nursing home
as day shook at you
with a pattern of pills.
You took notes up to the moment
the swimmers sopped up lake water
with yeasty towels.

Your reports were the nourishment
of our noon phone calls.
Sometimes I could not tell what
you were speaking of:
the number of swimmers that day
and the lake conditions
or the level of your pain
and the measurement of what you were giving up.

"Four, there were only four swimmers
today, but the lake was smooth as broth,"
You said, the day tuffs of your hair fell out.
Nests for water birds, you thought.

"Five today."
when your skin flaked off
moating in the lake air.
"The water is as warm as a dinner roll
and they did not need to dry off."

"One, only one swimmer."
The day numbness stopped your walking
and you gave your legs to the lake.
"There are white caps slicker than meringue."
Because they have my energy, you explained.

It happened so slowly
but there was less and less in the bowl
for our lunchtime talks.
I knew eventually I would be hungry
and all of you would be given to the lake
where swimmers start their day
wading through darkness.

SHIRLEY FERRIS

How shall we tell them
Marriage is like a garden
In all four seasons…

JEAN CARPENTER

Divorce Mississippi Style

The day was weird from the start.

Aunt Lou criticized my dress—said the polyester of red blue and
 yellow design was too short.
"You cannot go out in *that*," she said as she sat at my mother's
 kitchen table, shelling peas.
I knew the subtext was—"Why did you leave that young man, that
 good ole boy?"

I waited to blurt out
    "because he was screwing his teaching assistant"
but that blurt would not have been polite in my mama's kitchen. So
 I did not.
        I helped Aunt Lou shell peas instead. Bless her pea pickin'
        heart.

The phone rang. It was a boy friend from high school who heard I
 was back for a few days.
Did I want to go out for a coke?
You better believe I said yes before the ask was finished.

I slid into the booth across from him at the hamburger joint.
He ordered French fries with the cokes. We laughed and horsed
 around.
I always had fries with my Worcestershire sauce in those days—
 pretending the fries were steaks.
We drank and ate lustily. No alcohol—we were Bible belt and
 avoided that kind of moonshine.

The high school boy now man asked that I take a spin in his car like
 old times. I'm game.

Out on the highway on the way to Lake Shelby—or beyond, I'm not
 sure—we stopped.
The roadside park had benches, but we decided to walk into the
 woods. Sat on the forest floor.
    On pine needles and oak leaves.

Maybe Aunt Lou was right.
The needles did prick my thighs.
I didn't really care because
the sunlight danced on his.

LYNDA SCHRAUFNAGEL

On Broadway

All the young kids on Broadway are in their leather goods—
the girls with their noses pierced.
Black, such a somber color
which I myself prefer, and why not renounce
frivolity and try to live up to something
even if it's just the age one's in
and love.
A young couple, both of them beautiful,
the boy as much as the girl,
both studiously fashionable,
young and pouty with one another, young, as if it is—
and it is happening for the first time.
They'll break each other's hearts and wonder why—
of course I've lost it, that's the point, isn't it,
whatever it is, a second, third chance,
and with it, another pose to strike.

LONNY KANEKO

Falling Man
for J C

What's it like to climb a ladder and take a step
across the empty space between the rung and roof?
What act of faith the ladder will not slide
and the roof will have the will to hold your weight
as you ease from one embrace to another?

When you reach out and no one takes your hand,
can you assume that faith will bring a lovely stranger
to cradle you if you should slip and take a plunge
headlong into the abyss that awaits you and me
in the dream of an uneasy and uncertain sleep?

Even in the broadest day the snare is there,
an apparent safe and solid step, but blind confusion
for the unwary, who trusts someone's hammer hammered
nails true, that the roof is not glass, no mirage, but solid
as tar. Who among us will take the first step?

Our eyes deceive, subtle liars bent on playing
the mind like a fish on a fly. Too much line—
we recognize the slack; too little and we
sense the trap and snap the line. God, there must
be a god. Must falling be hook, line, and sinker?

In the middle of a fall, do you catch yourself,
send a signal to your brain crying "emergency!
Emergency!" or do the wrens stop chirping and people
stop talking? Does time signal time out?" "Time Out!"
you cry, your arms reaching out to embrace yourself.

Or do you give yourself to gravity, open
your arms as if to embrace the air? And dream the dream
of being a kite that hangs and flutters in the wind
as it winds its way toward the clouds? Or opening,
a parachute drinking air like a fat stomach?

Gravity always wins. Imagine stretching out
to greet it as it draws you in, curl and roll
as if gathering energy and releasing it
in a long rushing scream of white water.
Wherever there's pain there's still life.

Love wins and loses. Nothing's left
that's eternal. Every embrace has its limits.
Every hand has muscle, tendon, and nails.
What reaches out for you may not save you.
A falling man has few choices.

So you hope for pain and dread it. At first
there's nothing. No white spot to blind you,
no eyes to hold yours, no dark hole to fall into.
Man needs air before water, they say,
so the next breath is all we pray for.

Of Hands

Of hands, of
these hands, and
of the sea,
ever in all years
near.

Of hands their
own knowing of
the currents,
by grip and by
wash. Learning
feather, float, dive.
Learning squall.
What does a hand know?
That is not near
as touch, as want, as
dig, as
hold?
Against the furrow,
the frenzy, the
fit.

JULI GOETZ MORSER

The Timeless Shuffle

Ions
Fat as Cats
Rumble and bump
In the humid mid of night

We lie
Skin upon skin
Beneath the canvas ceiling
Of our summer home at water's edge

And when our calls
To the approaching storm
Recede
Nocturnal sounds preside

The smack of mallards sifting mud
The sploosh of a seal slipping off the raft
No songbirds but the startling honk of Canada Geese
Waves towing sand forming ridges in the rising tide

Ions from former lives caress
Recycled revived they are
In the churn of lovemaking
The remaking of life itself.

JILL BRADENFELS ANDREWS

Skagit Swing

And then the old guys
take the stage
dark suits and bow ties
the spotlight catches bifocals
bounces off balding heads
and slides down bright brass horns.

Trumpets, trombones, saxes lift
and out flows a sweet river of music
filling the room with sound-
String of Pearls and *Sentimental Journey.*

The men swing their shoulders
keeping the beat
they begin to shift shapes
slip right out of chunky bodies
into cool and easy.

They make music
like the young guys
they used to be
flippant and proud
sure of themselves
their sound breaking the hearts
of women on the dance floor.

JULI GOETZ MORSER

Gifts

Were it not
For the two fawns auburn
Standing
On the cut grass

Were it not
For the chartreuse
Nine o'clock
Midsummer light

Were it not
For your hand
Flopped across my hipbone
(Your silent acceptance of my unspoken apology)

Were it not
For the voice
Unnamed in each of us
(Mine pulls up along the black slip of my inside skin)

Were it not
Then I could not

Ask for the forgiveness
I owe
So many
Others

LONNY KANEKO

Body of Evidence

Here is the body of evidence laid out before us.
There across the floor are the shoes that left the prints.
And here and there are the hands, stretched open;
These are the culprits that did the deed, broke the window
And pulled open the closet, manipulated the safe
Where her heart had rested in the safety of imagination,
Reposing in the dark space that she called home.
Here under the jacket, in the chest, lay the intent
Of the perpetrator beating like a little drum, a battery,
That moved the hands and feet. And here, under my hand,
In this hard skull lie the plans he schemed into an intricate web.
Wrapped around him are the hand woven shawls
Created by the lawyers, meant to conceal the figure
Or shift the observer's eye from one shoulder
To another. These are the lines of the case.

We the jury sit impaneled in quiet isolation.
We have observed the heart pulled apart, its pieces placed
In evidence of callous intent. We have heard the argument—
How beauty raised passion like a stake in a heart, how love
Entered the equation, an X squared instigator of choice and action.
Did she say yes for passion or love? Did he offer love
To negotiate the contract, and renege on the obligation?
Did she offer her body and not her heart? And did he own
What she had offered? For in that night that he had attempted
Possession, she had clutched him to her breast
And wrapped him in her arms without a red ribbon.
Now we the jury are faced with the mirrors of deliberation,
To determine our place in this plot, how we share Intent,
Action, and punishment, to hang or be hung.

JULI GOETZ MORSER

Poem from Afar

Surfaces once smooth
Crack beneath
Reflective tissue
Behind mirrored glass

I feel aged lives
And follow them
Back
Burying deep
Like a velvet vole into my underworld

Legs thick
Immobile
With the weight of all the unseen
That I know

Yearning for soft arms
To wrap me
And roll me
Into heavenly light

Arch my backbone
Open my sternum
Let my heart
Ripen in rebirth

JANICE RANDALL

Crooked Road

Grief follows a crooked path
Winds down into valleys of despair
Climbs steep grade of acceptance
What do I know about such things?

Dreams bring past lives back
Awaken to find the empty place
Where youth and hope once resided
Follow the road; there's nowhere else to go.

CAL KINNEAR

Outside

this
weathered board cabin,
its cedar roof,
where Robert lived,
that's all it was, who
died. As if
I were waiting under trees,
ankle deep in leaves,
leaf-shadow-
dance.
With my braille fingers to brush
the words: they keep back
in shadow,
darkning-bugs, astir,
waiting
to be heard. No
saying
without listening, I listen
with my breath,
a late-evening air, mould-scent
of everything
that makes earth,
the burrow-words too, ghosts
from shadow, the close
clicking, the after-
thought, of blood.

JANICE RANDALL

Descent

She smells disaster.
Braces herself for impending disarray;
she pushes open the front door,
and holds her breath-
more from fear and dread
than the unmistakable scent of feces,
fear that this time will be the last.

Fresh urine burns her nostrils
deposits acrid saliva behind her tongue.
She steps around an overturned lamp
ignores Sunday's news scattered pages,
shattered light bulb.
spilled soup-roasted tomato-
slowly seeps orange and wet
into worn brown carpet.

She winces at hysterical helpless cries
emanating from gut wrenching
frustration, without words
every human act mission impossible.
She gathers broken shards
of life gone awry,
wipes up the muddled mess
that should have never been
as bittersweet tears
disappear into tangerine soapy muck.

She scrubs and scrubs
beyond need, past all obligation
while murmurs of comfort and care
take hysterics to silent jerking sobs.

Candles burn everlasting
Brahms in the background
Creates simulated, temporary peace.
Everyone wonders
when does life end
and Requiem begin?

LONNY KANEKO

Agoraphobia 1955

She pulls the front door shut
and turns the key until it's firm.
She pulls the blanket close and
stands behind the curtains,
watches the gauzy world move
past her window, and turns
the radio low.

Children play across the street;
they hit the ball into traffic.
Sometimes the ball hits
her window, rattles it like
a pigeon, lost and blind, flying
into glass, like a neighbor
wondering when and if
anyone is home.

When someone rings the bell
she sits in silence until
the steps retreat. The shades
are pulled; even at dusk
she keeps the room unlit
so no one passing by
will know how slowly
time can move.

Call screening keeps the voices
from the outside world
from entering past her phone.
She has had enough of visitors
who won't remove themselves.
Fingers in her ears will not
remove their cries.

Does she savor every
moment and every breath
of every second of every day?
Even in the dusk of living
the wrinkles accrue like taxes,
her hair a thinning testament
that life islanded against the world
is just a life.

LONNY KANEKO

Purple Heart

Since 78 she's fallen
once on the beach,
taken three stairs
and a header against a wall,
cracked three ribs,
been bruised from shoulder to hip
broken three fingers
seen them bent sideways
seen her kneecap shattered and
removed after a
tumble at the mall.

She's fallen on the neighbor's step
(another finger), too busy
talking, not watching,
a tumble on the grass
(thank god, nothing broken),
a collapse backward on the gravel
looking at the blue hole
in the sky, wondering,
who tipped the world?

A little tipsy not from drink
but toes that weave themselves
into a basket, cupped
like a Chinese tea cup,
toes crossed for luck?
no wonder twenty-eight
steps down to breakfast
every morning feels
like twenty-eight predators
preying for her.

MARY G. L. SHACKELFORD

February Prunings 2011

Before the immolation
before the uprising
the king of Tunisia
kept a wild tiger captive
in a cage. She was fed
live chickens every day.

In Yemen the median age
is seventeen and a half.
Unemployment is thirty-five percent.

And in Egypt a quarter million people
flood the ancient square by the Nile
throwing stones against the tyrant's thugs,
then in a surprising turn
embrace the military police
to join guard for
the libraries of Cairo.

Here in the Pacific Northwest
we cut twenty years' growth
a braided tangle
of wisteria and kiwi
to free the old cedar fence yearning
earthward held back only
by the vines' firm grip.

Fetching an essential tool, I round
the corner of the house. The sharp-shinned
hawk flies straight at my face
death screams of a robin
clenched in its talons.

I reach Barbara on the halls
of the Aberdeen hospital – last hours'
vigil for her mother.
We go out then to drum
the fading heartbeat.
She dies in the dark
before dawn. They rub her
body with olive oil and rose water.
Maureen had brought a crown of flowers.
I imagine their hands on the dead woman
body still warm and supple.
She looked so beautiful, Barbara whispers.

Today I go out to look at the world.
Behind the honeysuckle
the soft scattering of robin's feathers
dampened by moisture from the night
resists the drifting of the wind.

LONNY KANEKO

Rushing through the Gravel at 99

Picture this odd scene, little lady, no larger than a 5th grader,
Wearing sunglasses as wide as her face, hair tied up,
Until she is aerodynamics exemplified, crouched in her chair,

A little four wheeled sports car palpitating though the gravel,
Pausing to cross the handicapped lanes and dodging
Four door passenger cars as they push toward Genesee.

I am the motor and she the controller of brakes,
Pitching and stumbling, often at cross purposes,
Wind blowing through our clothes, almost out of control,

And fat little me, hanging on as the little chariot careens
From side to side when pick-ups and SUVs brush us back
To the sidewalk. In the day's moldering heat we stumble

Across traffic heading for the blue of the lake.
Like Icarus lured by the shape and fire of the sky,
"Let's do it," she says. "There's not much time left."

LONNY KANEKO

Violets for Mother

I hear my mother whose hips have
broadened sadly rocking in the chair
that she has reglued and tied together
twice these past five years.
She is staring through the living room,
older than her mother, her eyes fixed
on the glass that conveys the light and shade
of days. They are quiet now, straight lines
of sunlight that arrow to certainty and fear
enough to strap one to a rocking chair
for days on end as when she rocked me for ten
and my sister for some twenty years.
Now she rocks all my brothers, unborn
either through abstinence or luck.
Oh, that we could walk to her side or look into her face
and say that we love her
a chorus of our voices from Minidoka to Seattle
without unsettling the jungle
of African violets steaming quietly around her,
and in whose presence love
whispers its pink flowers.

SHIRLEY FERRIS

Always at housework
Mother hummed... I hear her now
through my own clenched teeth

LYNDA SCHRAUFNAGEL

Carnival

After my mother changes the diaper and powders
the rash spotting the delicate skin, she puts the baby
down in its crib. She's free now to head
for the kitchen, free to pop open a beer, to daydream
under the tick of the fluorescent light. On the table
the plastic peonies in a canning jar, Ben Franklin specials,
are nothing like those big flowers dotting the farmyard
where she grew up in the shadow of a white house,
the peonies fencing it, the sweet williams, and in the fields,
Indian paintbrush and black-eyed Susans she once dreamt
of running through with the boy in the storybook,
then the screen star pasted in a photo album,
then the handsome sailor home from war,
my drunk father who now barges in, who asks her to do it,
pushing that handsomeness toward her. And she says no.
So he brings up the girl he almost married,
the long-legged doll from the Long Beach carnival,
in love with sailors, in love with war. He brings up
the shotgun wedding, the nights she let him press her
to the seat of an old green pickup and the trap that came of it,
the hills of steel he shovels at Potascek's junkyard,
his second job. So he wants some fun. He wants
to waltz her across the linoleum floor, and he tries,
sliding into the walls papered with flowers, the chairs,
the kitchen counter where he grabs the greasy knife
and says he's only teasing, but a man does what
he has to do, and honey, he says, please, he says
as she takes her boots and coat and follows
the snow-plowed road the mile down
to her father's barn where the dark herd warms her
and the tails tick louder than they should,
and she thinks of the baby, she's left it behind,

even though this isn't what she wanted, to leave me,
her oldest, or years later, her other children, too.
She wanted to protect us as she protected herself,
to bundle us up and push us ahead into the stiff winter air,
or on summer nights, to shove us out the screen door first
and to circle the garden with us, the fields, as fireflies
lit up the dark carnival the nights had become.

LONNY KANEKO

Pre-Speech

My mother's face presses against mine afraid
that what I haven't said means I have nothing
to say, that the words she shares are garbled
in my brain, that I am mute because I hear
silence. She leans so close I can feel the heat
from her breath and words. She is afraid the future
will be an empty wall, that I will spend my days
believing that the wall is as full of life
as a book, or a zoo, or a school. Look at me,
she says, with love in her voice, but her
eyes fall away like channels I could fall into
and never return from. My father's voice rises
and falls in measured strokes, but anger measures
the metronomic rhythms, for he expects me
to be like him, to open my mouth, to engage
with others like cars rushing down the freeway
he drives me on. I know you think it's strange
a child without language can put these words for you
to read, but you can read my words in my face
and eyes. When you watch my eyes, they will touch
your face and slowly wander toward the window
where the words rise from my eyes and vanish in the glass.

C. HUNTER DAVIS

Sea Lions on the Warning Buoy

It is unpredictable when they
will howl,
a sound higher than my dog's
and as low as disappointment.
Sometimes it is when the waves
perfectly mangle the wind.
Water squeezes out the air and comes
clean to the shore
like a plan on a leash
that reaches its end.
Other times they bark when it is certain
the tide recedes.

They are the debris
from what didn't happen.
This flotsam of expectations
mounds together
They manage to ooze into shape
on the buoy that warns us
of our own dangers
and is just out of reason's
reach.

MARY G. L. SHACKELFORD

New Year

Pussy willows
Pink and silver – early,
Before the year turns.
Shirley brings them to the door.
I place them in a vase on the dining table.

My hands are growing old
In shape and strength
And lines etched into my skin
Pink and silver
Like ice worn long
Upon the water's surface
Contracting and expanding
With changes in the weather.

MICHAEL FEINSTEIN

        minus tide
        my hairline
        receding

ROGER DAVIES

deepening twilight—

going nowhere fast
on my exercise bike

ROGER DAVIES

When I'm Seventy

When I'm seventy
I'll take up the sax.

And put the strap
around my neck.

No photograph, please.
I don't want
my great grandchildren
imagining great granddaddy's
riff that never was.

When no one is listening
I'll try for that one note –
sounding, in my daydream,
something like OM;
Then I might wonder
about the surrounding
notes, around the one
I'm calling OM, and hope
to have out.

Opening the door
to reconsidering
the photograph:
My grand kids
penciling in,
on the back,
the explanatory note.

HELEN RUSSELL

he tells me the word
I'm looking for
total eclipse

INA WHITLOCK

Old Pants, Old Shirt

Abstraction of spattered paint
   on faded jeans, threads bare
   without repair, or remedy
   that time or negligence
   has put asunder.

Old shirt, elbow and cuff torn,
   stained dabs, smudges of color
   routing a map of years,
   tracing paint and hammer's
   where and when.

Old pants with raveled knee,
   not today's fashion
   but grime's humble work,
   clothes that still hold
   the scent of sweat.

Body's tactile energy
   manifest in cloth
   pulled from a plastic bag,
   slipping though fingers,
   last remains to throw away.

LONNY KANEKO

Clothes Make the Man

When we old men disrobe, we reveal what we truly are:
Indescribable humanoids, troglodytes and homunculi,
Neanderthals and missing links with hair like tufts of grass
Struggling to stay alive in beach sand populating the plains
Of aging backs. The ocean of skin is filled with rising islands,
The color of decaying humus. Beach balls, flesh-colored,
Stretched by heated air, contain the body's lardy hubs,
Their blow holes tied and protruding like pregnant women's
Belly buttons, wide as fifty-cent pieces. Every bottom sags
Like two deflating balloons wrinkling in the cooling breeze.
As if hanging from strings, they barely bob, but clench
So they squeeze and droop like the cheeks of aging peaches
Molding on a window sill. Human bling hangs,
A variety of lengths, some placed so delicately
They are almost invisible, receding into fern filled,
Dank caves. No joy-filled sight, these bodies on spindly legs,
Knobby arthritic knees, needing aluminum walkers and canes,
Struggle into chinos and socks, shirts and jackets and ties.
But when they stand, wrinkles disappear; their poplins creased
And clean, they comb what's left, put on their glasses
And face their feminine partners, who embrace their lovers,
clean, handsome, and civilized with horizon-wide smiles.
They affirm the old rule about men and their clothes.

ANN SPIERS

Kitchen Help

In the outdoor kitchen,
she stands by her bucket of chlorine water.
Her hands, in latex gloves, pull two hundred forty
basil leaves from their stems, only those leaves
willing to stand up straight
next to the one-hundred-twenty collapsed tarts.

No matter the task,
she is the night kitchen. She keeps
her fingers going while looking out
to see day escape downhill through the tea roses,
and night deepen around the lights, and hear
chatter fill the dining tent.

Dessert out,
she cleans her station, and as the last plates return,
carried in the outstretched arms of servers,
it is done.

She takes home a quart of lavender ice cream,
and eats it in the velvet of her solitude.

JILL BRADENFELS ANDREWS

dishes in the sink
house full of silence
grandchildren gone home

SUSAN GRAY WILEY

Angel Wings

Angel Wing Plants
given starts from a friend
will grow, I know.

Expectations in newly potted soil
withered all too soon
forgotten, as dead.

Too busy to throw out the mess,
it sat in the West
white chipped window frame
witness to setting suns,
winter rain, and backyard weeds.

So much time in molded sod
to stir and struggle
life revealing
through cell, root, stem
and finally tiny upshoot leaf.

Now in the East white frame
convoluted burgundy red soars
with earthgreen spotted wings.

Graced above earth toward sunrise
upwards in flight and foolery
Testimony
to the forgotten.

CATHERINE JOHNSON

May Swim off the Coast of Clare

There were three of them
Sisters
Running naked in wild serpentine loops
Along the beach
frisky as ponies
They chased one another
Shrieking and shouting, sometimes in Irish,
Calling their names in the bright chill air
The littlest one pumping her arms – just to keep up

Meanwhile a dark haired mother
Walked behind
carrying the clothes.
When she reached the black rocks
She made neat piles:
tucking socks into shoes, folding pants on top, shirts
jumpers next, panties last
Always keeping one eye on the water's edge

Before they came, I had been dozing, a sweet vacationer's sleep,
Tucked from the wind, in a hollow of sand and weathered stone
Dressed in wool and zipped jacket, I lay warm and smiling when I
    heard them

Sitting up and blinking my eyes against the glare, and
such innocent beauty – the wildness of long limbed youth,
black manes shining against the soft green hills
running breathless and warm and brave enough
"Mamma" the littlest one called, "watch me, I'm a mermaid."
It was she who led her older sisters into the dark green waters of the Sea.

In that moment I measured my years
Who I had once been and who I had become
The sight of them made me weep, and smile, and weep some more.

SUSAN GRAY WILEY

Cheli La Pass - Bhutan

Mist mixes prayer with flags
dead voices rise,
surmount, surround, choke
in wind-snap to the brain

Threads slap threads strong
against stormed out fringe
sound deafening all thought
white on weather white

Wet drinks up flags,
drips to stay afloat
a life, a death, a ghost

I walk among hundreds, thousands
ducking each soul
Repeating words long flown
to all sentient beings

There are many ways
to kiss the sky.

SUSAN GRAY WILEY

Mt. Rainier

Wearing morning sun
    like Apollo's crown
The mountain calls all climbers
    to its weathered face.

Measured plans and calculations
    they accept
Carrying survival as appendage
    into another time.

Leaving meadowed Trillium
    in rivulets of Lily
For angled ice of glacier rock
    split and hung to freeze
    in silence.

Pace slows, keeping time
    through crunching crystalled
  light
Like respectful deer
    they feel vibrations.

Only dark brings rest and tents
    set on mountain belly rumblings
Distant avalanche
    of one's own vulnerability.

Moon ices snow in blue
    assent climbers prepare
Marmots watch
    as they shadow away.

Step upon step
    heart pounding heart
        breath inside breath
        focused together
        one intent
        never broken

Until dawn and summit wind
    of unexpected vision.

Time smoothes all footsteps
Yet marks of white etch upon souls
    Its own design.

PAUL BACKSTROM

Landmarks

Steam from a sun-warmed fence
Dead branches leaved with dewy webs
Hill not quite seen in whiteness

What I remember
    won't lead me back

MICHAEL FEINSTEIN

the way rain begins,
or the maple adds a ring—
slowly growing old

ROGER DAVIES

dark clouds
over chimney corners—

lucky raindrops
scurry into Crystal

ERIC HORSTING

Opening Nights

Something must then begin, they say, gestures
perhaps: the imperative's all, the sure walk
through the false door on cue, the stark memory
of the words no one else can speak only
you can repeat, to perfection, they say,
loving you for it. And after it's done
again, you flick the collar of your cloak
up against the cold and dark and you walk
down the cobbled streets of the ancient port
standing for a time on the dock, staring
at the stars like no others, as they seem
to you then; and you observe one fall,
as happens, and decide once again, as you
have before, that the event means no more
than it is, light streaming suddenly down,
and this decision comforts you again,
so that you end your evening tracing
the streets to home, its rue, its familiar door.

JANICE RANDALL

North Beach Sunday

Early morning fog shrouds cathedral spires
Wet grass soaks canvas shoes
Empty park bench left bereft
Catatonic without stern Italian grandmothers
Chattering Chinese locals
And black clad monsignors.

Ghosts of childrens' laughter
Skitter across rain-slick sidewalks
Smudged pink hopscotch boxes
Memories left behind yesterday's sun-soaked afternoon
Slides and swings hang still and heavy
Reticent under lackluster heavy flannel sky.

Church bells clatter, shatter solitude
Early devotees scurry through massive doors
Car beeps pierce woolen silence
beneath Sunday's single ray
City sleeping by the Bay awakens slowly,
Coffee, homemade bread and garlic
Wafts tempting tendrils into every empty space.

And so a new day begins in North Beach.

JILL BRADENFELS ANDREWS

fat bellied rain clouds
heron on the beach below
all-weather feathers

MICHAEL FEINSTEIN

morning without wind
sea mist fills
the foxglove bells

ROGER DAVIES

Nostalgia

I have come to the attic
to prepare my mind and feelings
for writing the poem
that's getting ready to emerge
after I look in the old trunk
and see the faded tan photograph
of my father standing
next to the 38 Ford,
with his bride to be,
my mother, the warm wind blowing
the wisp of her then black hair
out from beneath the bandanna
she had tied, that early summer
day, over her head. They had
gone to the beach
where my grandparent's
once swam. They had put
aside the cares of the day,
and sought, in swimming,
what their parents had found,
and I find myself pleased to be
looking out the little attic window
at the lawn below,
and not getting into the trunk
at all, leaving the faded photograph
poem to emerge for someone else.

MARTA COU

Nostalgia Habanera

The water
Is cleansing and beautiful and crystalline.
It holds things in its depths
We cannot see
that thrive in spite of us,

And it separates
Me
From that
which I Love
Almost
Most.

SHIRLEY FERRIS

planting carrots ~
I kneel at the altar of
ordinary life

ROGER DAVIES

The Surface

Spring sunshine and the puck
is through the ice.

What we passed, careened,
and shot, hurrying to catch,
rests in an ice-skimmed sketch
with leaves and needles.

A small tableau has deked us:
a puck is a puck
and something else,
just below the surface.

ANN SPIERS

It's snowing. Again.
Indian plum half dangling.
John Browne plays the blues.

INA WHITLOCK

Moon Over Snow

Giver of light in a world of cold
    come to ease a frost of ignorance,
    to warm dark corners of repose
When lights go out, and no wired heat,
    no food is warm for comfort,
    only the white coverlet outdoors
Glows in silence of the snow.

JEAN AMELUXEN

Across the floor
the sun
marks winter's progress

ROGER DAVIES

Michigan January

Winter...

snows
swirl around
cottages

and sweep
across frozen
Crystal.

In the silent
rooms
of our childhood

the summer air,
cold now,
ventures slowly
outside

mingling
with white waves.

ANN SPIERS

>
> Burton Coffee Stand
> debating who's most Vashon
> How new you all are!

KAJIRA WYN BERRY

Adventure beckons
but oh! how sweet, familiar
ordinary ways

CAL KINNEAR

Klompen Clogs
(for Trimpin)

In the gallery hangs a curtain of wooden clogs.
The magician makes them klomp an eerie dance, a Totentanz of joy.

They don't move. They sway a little in the air.
Where is the dance? I can't keep still.

I remember the grief of Maria Schell as Grushenka,
her eyes ringed with kohl.

Her smile weeps. Her love spills out of her
from her mother's grief, and *her* mother's.

A sea butterfly begins life in the sea as a man
and only in time matures to a woman.

I want to wear these clogs and dance.
I want in me this grief of a woman's joy.

I want to go out,
my eyes ringed with kohl.

MICHAEL FEINSTEIN

sleepless night
a patch of moonlight
crosses the bedspread

MARY G. L. SHACKELFORD

Full Moon in April

Night slips into
my tossing dreams.
Frogs in full throat.
From the ravine
two courting great horneds
bay at the moon.
Though clouds cover the light
my blood churns
to the magnetic pull
of creative
unrest.

MARY G. L. SHACKELFORD

Halfway to Spring Equinox

It is a good merry morning.
The brown grasses, flattened
by winter's settling gravity,
lift and stir in the gusting
wind which is at once
balmy and bodacious.
Hyacinths and hellebore
bloom by my door,
and the itinerant Michael has come
from his lair in the Okanagan
for his 23rd year of tree care on Vashon.

I have been expecting his knock.

His handshake is warm and
his gaze steady in my eyes
when I invite him inside.
He brings in the honest scent
of his life, sweat and the faint sweetness
of sap newly rising to the snip
of his sharp tools, infrequent
baths and a single change of dry clothes.

Today he will prune the plum and the apple
the pear and the apricot.
When he is gone, I will go out. Gather
his leavings, the sheddings that open
space for new fruit.
Perhaps there will be a few sticks
to make *ikebana* for the house.

I will bring them inside
to bloom in the hours, days, years
of warm light stored in tree rings,

sunshine released now from firewood
we burn on the hearth.

It is a good merry morning.
The brown grasses, rested
from winter's downward pull
lift and stir.

ROGER DAVIES

The Matters-at-Hand

The Queen Anne's Lace
is bending and bowing
with the wind,
mixing it up
with the flit-about dragonflies
hovering here, then there,
sometimes teaming up
in a airborne dragonfly tango
and keeping their 30,000 eyes
on the matters-at-hand.
And up the hill
from this small meadow
the theology students
at The Atlantic School of Theology
keep their two eyes each
on the pages
of exigesis and midrash,
while down below,
at our meadow,
the white flowers,
psalmists of the breeze,
circulate the sweet air.

JULI GOETZ MORSER

What Morning Brings

Tide's grabbling fingers
Creep up the naked shore
Spilling into barnacle shells
That sprout a single feather into the chilling water

Circling winds weave
Through wafting fir boughs—
A breath for mother earth

Waking in our simple tent at harbor's edge
Doors open to the gathering day
I tumble from a night of wresting thoughts
To see a single blue heron standing starkly still
On our undulating raft

Quiet, watchful, patient for breakfast
Its tall form
Held
In a spotlight of the rising sun.

CATHERINE JOHNSON

Waking

There is nothing sweeter than
curling with you between waking and dreaming.
The heat of your steady fire burning through the night
warming my back,
Your arm wound 'round me holds me close
and yet, when the need to move, turn over, or stretch - stirs in me
you let go; the way you would release
kite to the wind, string running out, waves running in.
Such letting go is a kind of blessing, a grace.
We sleep this way, so full of trust,
both tethered and free

MARTA COU

Longing

I miss that place
where my head fits
just under your arm
when you sleep,
after we have loved each other
to exhaustion.

I miss the sound you make in your peaceful slumber,
like a steady, far-away train,
while I listen,
content to have my arm
wrapped 'round the rise and fall
of your soft warm belly.

JILL BRADENFELS ANDREWS

Your Odyssey

Like Penelope waiting for Ulysses
I sit at home waiting for you to return from your odyssey,
only your goal is to ski the snowy Rockies,
not rescue a wayward wife or explore distant islands.

You sailed off not in a boat but in your Toyota 4-wheel drive,
not on the wine-dark sea but on Interstate 5,
a charcoal-colored highway that unrolls its yellow line
replacing the need for celestial navigation.

Your Scylla and Charybdis are semi-trucks and black ice.
Your Circe is the sultry babe leaning on the bar,
smiling at you after your exhilarating day on the slopes.
In Colorado no goddess Calypso
will offer you eternal life if you accept her hand.

Meanwhile I am by the woodstove not weaving but knitting
an intricate Irish sweater, just for you. I click my needles
instead of thumping the shuttle of a loom.
Unlike Penelope I have no need to unravel it each night
to forestall advances of one hundred and eight suitors.

I have no resident son to keep me company
and ward off solicitations. Instead my faithful dog
lies at my feet and barks at every outside sound.
He is keeping me safe for your homecoming.

INA WHITLOCK

Travel

You pulled the luggage of your life
    on wheels of time through fog
to leave me at the ferry dock.
    Your early morning shave
soft lingered on my chin, a kiss
    a hug, your passport held.
Your mind and body leaving here
    as you walked down the plank—
a passage too far to see.

ERIC HORSTING

Damaged Goods

1

You bring me white pants from the secondhand
store. I give up my jeans; cotton feels so good
in summer. One day, as we pitch the tent
at the curving shore, I forget—no, don't care—
and kneel to hammer a stake. It's late; the sun's
gone. My knee's stained with grass and mud.

2

I bring you leather shoes from the factory
outlet. You kick off your sneaks; real hide breathes
so your feet won't sweat and freeze in winter.
You polish those shoes, once a week, for about
a month, but soon the slush and sidewalk
salt stain the uppers and eat at the soles.

3

We find a house. It's spring. The weeds surround
the stone foundation, the cement porch steps
crumble, and inside, cobwebs prepare the air
for spiders, the grimy bathtub leaks through
the plaster ceiling; after one look around,
we skip and grin. "It's ours," we say, "It's ours."

JEAN CARPENTER

My Best Things

"Love covers a multitude of sins," my mother said.
I always attributed that saying to her in my speeches.
To my surprise, I learn that St. Paul or somebody else
said it in the Bible first.
My mother never attributed; perhaps she thought I
would just "know" who said it first.

She also had other sayings, some I can't fix origin of –
such as, "We have enough food for Cox's army."
Who was Cox and where was this army anyway?
Was the food good?

My favorite sayings she gave freely and often included these:
"Have an attitude of gratitude" and
"You'll feel better if you do something for somebody else."
But my very favorite saying she said most often late in life
and again on her last life day.

She looked up at my brother and me
from her lovely bed smoking her virtual cigarette
(she'd want you to know she started smokin' when
it was a sin and not a health hazard) and said:
"You are the best things I ever did."

The best things? Over her teaching, her loving, her cooking
her twelve stepping, her politicking, the seafood gumbo and the
black bottom pies?! We were the best things.
I didn't really know until now what she meant.

My politicking, administrating, loving, justicing (no fancy dishes
on this list)—all of these pale to my best things.
I hope my best things know I feel the same way about them
that my mother felt about my brother and me.
My very best things.

KATE JOHNSON

Septima
For my dad: The things that took an extra line to say

I'm trying to remember the moment
in which I first decided to live
Sometimes, I've been asked
What I believe is real?
Or am I afraid
Of the dark? And I wonder
Are those the sorts of things we choose?

I turned four in a house we chose
For potential energy, for possible momentum.
As you fling me toward our third-story ceiling, I almost wonder
If I'll come down alive?
I'm only a little afraid
After all, I, asked.
And I never thought you'd drop me, really.

I remember feeling real:
Hair wet, and dripping glacial melt, you let me choose
Our freeze-dried dinners, and gravely ask
If we should change our socks. There comes a moment
When I tell you, "I'm afraid"
And you laugh and say "no wonder,"
"You're alive."

I'm staring down the rest of my life
A thousand words, and visions to make real
I look up, and choke with wonder
And barely, almost, believe I get to choose.
You arrive with the flowers, and I know that this time, you're afraid
Do you know, or do you want to ask
What I think of this moment?

Sometimes, now, I stand in the sun as I dial your number, I love that moment
You answer, I know what you'll say. You'll tell me it's my life
And when you're living, it's okay not to know, it's okay to ask
What's real?
I'll watch the leaves go gold against the sky, and you'll tell me not to be afraid.
You'll tell me not to wonder
If I deserve to choose.

Do you remember if you asked me to choose
If I wanted to be real?
I wonder
Was I afraid?
Well, I'm afraid of chance, and chaos, and mabye of the dark. But of life?
I don't think so. I think you asked, and I answered
The moment you caught me.

MARGARET HELDRING

Schoolhouse on Vashon

I am like a wagon train
Moving across the prairie.
I carry wicker chairs and
Grandmother's portrait,
Old pots and kettles.
My dog perks her ears, lifts her nose.
She's caught a scent.
For so long, home was over the horizon,
On the other side of rising mountains and
Roaring rivers to ford.
I move under the soft blue sky
Past wheat grain waving at us.
Soon, my sons and I will stop
To rest, and light the evening fire.

ANN SPIERS

>
> ever-bearing strawberries
> grandma buckets water
> out of the wading pool

JULI GOETZ MORSER

March 14

From above
It looks like scratches on ice
Little shavings fluffed to one side
From the edge of a skater's blade

But really
It's just moisture condensed.

Between it and the ultra-sheer blue
We fly, and higher even
Space takes hold inking the atmosphere
Like a possessive octopus

The sun
Still tall in Seattle
Breaks across the scudded
Scuffed surface

Which really
Is just moisture condensed.

I wonder if I have it
This moisture
Condensed like clouds across my
    cheekbones
So high up my eyes tear

Thinking
Wanting
Her wrap of warmth
Knowing

And now at 50
Loving

That the wrap I seek
I'll soon give
My mother
On this her 80th birthday.

SUSAN GRAY WILEY

A Run

Mother and Colt run
    a wave through pasture grass

Run new bone in
    gleaming muscled elegance
    contoured to one.

Run juxtaposed joy
    flank to flank
    sweat on sweat
    weaving together
    wet polished shine

Run in moment
    as wave turns
    momentum to importance
    uniformity to identity.

Mother knew to nudge her son
    Awake
from lazy noonday sun.

JILL BRADENFELS ANDREWS

perched on the porch rail
kingfisher rattles me
into now

JANICE RANDALL

Roses in the Snow

Scarlet roses lie in the snow
Like the blood
cold in her veins
      Endless tears flow.

Her lips frozen in time
Silenced by hatred
      and the lies he told.

Wind whispers through tall firs
Tells short stories
of the life
she once knew
belief and trust
long gone
      where all hope fled.

Eyes close
Against harsh morning light
Scent of roses
      Fill winter air.

EDEEN PARISH

An April Day
In Memory of Paul
19 April 2009

Air still crisp from the winds
Of winter blowing over the snows
Of Mount Olympus; the Sun, brilliant
In a Bird's egg blue Spring sky...
   A day bursting with April!

A longed for Spring Day,
Spilling over with life: Tulips and
Plum blossoms; bees working,
Birds checking out new nesting sites—
   A day made *for living...*
Not for leaving!

But you left, unannounced,
Casting off the shroud of pain that
Long tormented you, shedding
The dark, heavy garment,
Leaving all behind.

You took this bright day
With suddenness, with non-reversing
Permanence in the choice you
Made, leaving those who love
You filled with sadness.

Be at Peace, Paul,
May the knowledge of your
Hard won freedom from pain
Help soften the grief
Of your going...

Go in Peace, Paul
On your journey into
The great Beyond.
Peace...Peace.

JULI GOETZ MORSER

Pastels

Answers sought
In boxes and books
Begging
From friends, lovers, my parents
Do not work the same designs
That once they did

Now I see
Pain as ribbons
The dark side inside
Is colored pastels

It's not the answers
Anymore
But the measure of distance traveled

It's the searching
The questions
The seeking itself

That make my ribbons wrap
Like bright colorful banners
Across a thin transparent sky
Round the earth
That girth
Of all we think we know for sure

CATHERINE JOHNSON

For Jacinta

My friend, Jacinta, had
Dark chocolate hands
She waived them like signal flags across the campus square.
Up, down, this way and that, snapping overhead...
With her head thrown back and a hold your belly laugh echoing
    from within
To be greeted by her
Was to taste the original flavor of welcome.

My friend, Jacinta, had
Days that were full
She kept appointments the way others keep journals
Meetings with friends, meetings with students, meetings with
    colleagues, meetings with strangers...

Jacinta made time – expand.
She could blow into a room, like a hot wind
burning the brush of injustice or ignorance.
She could sail lazy too,
closing her office door with a quiet click, saying
"Un huh," and I know,"
to my various complaints and confidences.

My friend, Jacinta, had
A throw your head back, grab your belly kind of laugh

My friend, Jacinta, had
Warm dark eyes
You could pour them over pancakes, over grief or good news
You could pour them over an annual budget statement making it
    sweeter that way.
Jacinta's eyes could laugh, could flash, could dance.

Jacinta's eyes are closed now
her days unhurried
her waving hands finally still

My friend Jacinta died
today.

INA WHITLOCK

Blue Glass

Sparkle of blue glass in sand
    that I reach for, but cannot find,
    blue, the color of your eyes,
washed smooth with stones,
    bronzed bits, bottles broken,
        opaque as our years together
            when we called this beach ours.

MARY G. L. SHACKELFORD

Uncovered Ground

My garden
Untended since midsummer
Grows wild –
A cornucopia of fruits
All bound up and hidden
In the tangle.
From my bedroom,
Tucked into the high limbs
Of the madrone's shelter,
I contemplate the brown
And dying profusion.

A sunny day –
Veteran's Day it is –
We clear the massed
And matted vegetation
Lay bare the earth
And turn the soil over.
Exposed ground rests,
Fallow and unseeded.
Wild geese fly
The Taurus moon wanes
And rocks sing.

Before the turning of the light,
Between the candle and the flame
I and thou
Rest in silent stillness,
Uncovered ground.
This moving benediction,
Invisible threads woven around us,
Opens a wordless communion

So utterly different
From what we usually share:
The possibility and struggle
Of silent ghosts in shared territory –
Unwitting participants who lead us
Into the halting exploration
Of each other's company.

SUSAN GRAY WILEY

Wrapped Up

Wrapped tight in waterproof plastic skin
I venture out of car up ferry boat stairs
"Life Jackets can be found under seats"
wails recorded garbled precautions

Through finger greased windows
clear water calls over gulls
crying deep in my cells of cellulose
to play, dive deep
push hard off bottom
cut waves
bloody up soft elbows
wear revised Jackets for Life

I stare at worn experienced boots
pointing different directions

following the proper boot
to landing horns
I safely buckle up.

ANN SPIERS

The Great Blue Heron
calculates its next strike
ferries late again

JILL BRANDENFELS ANDREWS

Afflicted

Worry rodents gnaw at my thoughts,
chewing corners of my plans,
shredding serenity with tireless stirring.
Their snouts snoop and rummage,
invading my care for loved ones.
They tread on my travel plans,
revel in possible peril.

Whiskers twitching, long teeth nibbling,
they borrow trouble.
In their nests they lie in wait,
naked tails curled, bright eyes watchful,
eager for new morsels.
They poke into the stack
of daily reflections,
rustle through social inadequacies
and tactless comments.

They find delicacies without number
in the clutter of my mind.

C. HUNTER DAVIS

Going

When I do not want to go,
I go by familiarity

Or some bad habit

until I merge .
.
I pause at every stop to check and see
if I still have myself
because I am easy to lose
especially when I want
someone else's self . .

I stop again to see
if I am there
even when I know where I am going
     when I am directed but do not have directions.

I force myself
to overhaul myself
even when I feel no need to stop
     when I've contributed to another
     and can not stop contributing
     when I've limited myself
     and can not stop limiting.

Going, I'm told, is good for the heart, going faster even better
unless there is no stopping .
Misunderstanding runs along the side because
the stops are so light, they're s as easy to miss
as witch hazel's first winter bloom.

LONNY KANEKO

Beasts From the Heart

1
They're here tonight as they always are,
waiting for us to enter their private dark,
their muzzles gray with the digging
that pervades their lives.
They are content to spend their lives
in afternoons that hold no more than dreams.
When we sleep, they test their voices
against the night's blind disorder.

2
I enter the cave, and the mind's voice
heats the soft fat of my childhood.
My stutter shuts off the world
and insures my isolation.
Nothing exists. The eye
mirrors the self. Where
does the beast begin?
As the central figure in the play
it enters disguised
in a house dress, long black hair
rolled into a bun, a tongue
sharp as a row of needles.

3
In December my mother snarled
when she meant to smile. I curled
bear-like in the cave of their lives.
I have sniffed the dank reaches
of the undergrowth.
I have seen the tunnels of moles and gophers.
The blind wanderings of prescient worms
have led to the central root that fed
the barbed circle of her words.

4
Is it enough that the beast
should roll in it and dust my nose in it—
this abstraction of dirt I wear?
The cold is not cold until I admit it;
heat is never sweltering until the mind perspires;
and pain—the cut does not bleed until I look
for blood; the body is too ready
to comply with what the mind desires.

5
Outside the chain-link
preserve is a world for hunters
who reserve the hours between midnight
and dawn to drift into the lives
that surround them. I feel the brush
of wilderness against my thigh.

Midnight! The people who love
me enter their own nightmares;
the chains are lifted,
and I revert to the invisible hunter.
When I howl the world descends.

RON SIMONS

Mail to my dentist
Using the regular stamp
Not the funny one

HELEN RUSSELL

of some use after all
grandson asks
what's a split infinitive

JANICE RANDALL

The Laundress

She carries her burden lightly most days
hoists the familiar tattered basket,
lets it rest comfortably in the notch
of her upper right pelvic bone
where her babies
once contentedly rode.

Laundry, life's obligatory duty
woven tightly into her DNA
give thanks for perma-press, knits and modern casual
she rarely brandishes an iron,
the metal antiquity languishes upright
behind a row of musty coats
until weddings
or funerals demand.

No back-breaking iron washtub for her generation
reserved supremely for childhood fun
no ringer works, washer woman whirligig
washer deluxe, wonder washer
speed queen, happy home steam washer
or American beauty-
Woman's friend has come a long way…
launderettes a blessed
distant
memory.

But duty remains, relentless.
gathering
sorting
spinning
drying
folding
stacking
repeat.

She delights in forgotten coins
and lost buttons found
wonders at the mystery of missing socks
swears at the disastrous blue bleeding pen
stains, rips, wear and fade
reveal subtle secrets and quirky habits
she observes the wearer of each item distinctly
listens to tales told thread by thread
teenage adventures, her husband's exploits
in the old man's clothes most of all,
ancient moments washed away
and recreated every day.

Solace found in repetition
zen-like mantra
quiet love gift
rote comfort
cleanliness next to godliness
generation to generation
Thank god
for the goddess
of laundry.

CAL KINNEAR

An Other Eye

Here I am again, daymind
in my little dory bobbed up from nocturnal splendor
and slough,

a little tipsy from an old knee.
I keep Dream Time like a separate clock,
like an Other,

crossed, eye, the pressure on the eyeball,
a warp pressure on sight passing slant through
ordinary time,

as on the hero Cuchulain's one needle eye.
The water sparks under the flint,
gay wind.

A covey of gulls busies on the muck-tide shore.
If I didn't brace myself against the dock rail
I would fall,

with a tearing eye, for a time
always just lost, as
just found.

ROGER DAVIES

What to Do With Political Ideas

Ideas like flags
flapping on a hill.
Brought down
and stood on.
No pure air
no pure sunlight
no raised fists
between us
and the flag
and the earth beneath.
No pledges
of allegiance –
in time,
let it
cover our shoulders
cradle our babies
provide shade
and privacy
one room to the next,
and in the month
of harvest,
gather into itself
the garden's gifts.

CAL KINNEAR

(The Names)

There was a reason
the Names were not spoken,
kept dream, kept
under the tongue
for the uncertain times.
Spoken, they
lumbered out into the world,
cathedrals and palaces,
jumbo jets that used to fly,
museums now,
a wonder to children.
There will not be
any more. They are gone
the gods.
We wasted them.
We will have to make do
with dust and water and
the rubber of spent tires. And
the silence
between.

ROGER DAVIES

Unclear Cut

It is not clear,
can not be clear,
in our single-minded minds,
what the cut does.

On the surface
clear sounds better
than cloudy
better than murky
better than obstruction
"there was something
in our way"

The man looks
out his new window
across the newness of
the single-minded lawn
saying
"we couldn't see the
ridge over there,
but now we do"

in a language
the birds who
flew through
the dense of the forest
didn't speak

nor the deer
who could dream at night
beneath the fullness
of the dreaming trees.

C. HUNTER DAVIS

Communities

Halfway up our afternoon,
(the shared sandwiches gone
and our talk emptied on the trail)
trees gather.
The hemlock choreographs
into the parsimonious fir who offers
nothing to the cedar chorus line
though they rub roots.

This is community; of trees.
They do not encourage
embrace. Their admiration is for
the efficacy against the wind.

C. HUNTER DAVIS

Embrace

The madrone roasts its skin in the fire.
The stone pine spits its pitch beneath the flames.
The alder drops the fungal flavor on the forest.
The field where the silver maple grew
flows into the hearth,
drizzled with meadowsweet and common yarrow.
The cedar donates its rain dried mystery
without protest.
The papered peel of river birch wanders generously into smoke.

The nuggets of heat are given as offerings
from these woods
from the wolf willow sprouted in creeks
from the tight mesquite toughed by drought
from the hard scrub oaks stiff from wintering.

They massage so gently into warmth,
slip so unambitiously into carbon
their exchange so benevolent,
it is almost unnoticed.

ROGER DAVIES

Leaf Bud Futures

The Beeches the year, as every year,
are playing for their future.

They are the big league movers
in commodities, brokering deals
with sunlight and soil.

They know which way
the wind is blowing.

When most birds fly south
they're the ones with the patience,
waiting for next summer's
bullish exuberance,
when everything
can't help but
come up green.

But now
looking at the falling leaves
sinking to new lows,
they see the growth potential
and dig in.

And in the spring
at the opening bell
of dawn,
they've already
got their buy order in.

CAL KINNEAR

Turning Color

It's no use sitting home by the fire,
adding the sticks of wood one at a time,

watching the flames flicker and writhe, keeping warm.
It'll end in a heartbeat, same as it began.

The foliate trees are ablaze, and some long-stalked plant
I don't know the name of with bat-eared leaves.

What was deep and humble maroon
is today a dense red flame.

I know in my breath the feel of turning color,
a slight chill, a gift is coming,

a little flock of cedar waxwings with their crests and masks
come sudden into the cotoneaster to feast

on the fermenting red berries
in this frailing, thread-bare season.

INA WHITLOCK

Christmas 2010

Oh Christ, why do I hesitate
to feel joy this Christmas
or celebrate one birth so long ago,
or sing tender songs of Bethlehem
when mortars and lethal drones
drop death, and men crave killing?

The burning bush of Moses
and the shining star,
a pagan Christmas tree and snow
at the sacred core of Christmas.

Simple story obscured in myth
of birth miraculous, no pain
or lust, or sensual delight,
yet poverty and hunger cries
the same as when the angels sang
and we still sing, but once a year,
the time when grace is found
in a mother and her baby's smile.

No Christmas hints of sacrifice,
body, mind, or hands nailed,
when Christian soldiers kill
and die, defending what?
A Crusade to save the world,
the dollar and democracy
by buy. buy, buying Christmas—
though the only true gift is
Love, and love for everyone.

A tinseled star atop my plastic tree,
ragged refugee, packed and unpacked
half a century, still awaits the essence
of Christ's Holy Night and Peace.

SUSAN GRAY WILEY

Turn It Down

Turn down the volume, please
Too much weight on ears
no comprehension of
"The shooter blew himself to bits."

Turn up sounds on moon tides
surging empty shores
Turn up clam spit, feeding cilia
wings stretching back on Cormorants
gulping winter sun
I need to hear muscled Pilings crack,
open then shut
to descending dark.

Turn up shouts
of Amarillis growing
I cannot miss its bud or pink

It takes fine tuning to hear
a baby turn
in its womb
or cry before birth.

INA WHITLOCK

Too Much

Information comes and goes
    flows everywhere in languages
       enveloping the planet in
Excess of noise, cacophony,
    Decibels of rage or calm
       tones magnetic waves
Bombarding atmosphere, a
    clamorous overreach of
       Channels cellular and cells,
Information over mind,
    illusion of fact as reality
       no subtle silences to end
All inclusive macro sounds
    Too much to absorb
       absolve or comprehend.

ROGER DAVIES

Information

Just arrived, twenty containers of Info:
dockside, freeze-dried.
Expire date stamped on the pallets,
ready for distribution. Universally,
equitably, everyone gets the recommended
dosage. The shipment comes
regularly. Irregularities screened for,
we never need now to ask for more.

INA WHITLOCK

Thumb Power

Power of hand held images,
indulgence of he next
and the next possible text—
vicarious, virtual streams,
pixels, pictures, cyber fields,
harvests burning in the palm.

Informational waves, minds
lost from spirit's accord,
dismembered messages that
form on screens to disappear,
too small to see, to quick
to reason textual intent.

Thumb power ripping time
from warp of memory,
old paradigms lost
in soundbites, flash drives, surf,
catching the unwary
in digital high tide.

ANN SPIERS

Lavender Harvest
(to Vashon Island's Lavender Sisters)

Lavender blue and rosemary green,
When I am king you shall be queen.
Nursery Rhyme

i
Our crew-lead, over and over,
counts lavender bunches
      soaking in plastic tubs
      (Grosso. Royal Velvet.)
calling out to us: yes 350 yes 50 to go.

Dawn. July.
Lavender blue dilly dilly.
The rooster is in training,
his cock-a-doodle-doing
stutters, fades,
then starts up again.

Scent fills the morning chill,
memories of pale purple tint,
stored silk and satin, of cures
for loss of voice and lack
of nerve, wound dressings,
and oh my love.

Through the rows,
a shy acre of blue haze,
guys collect bunches
from the humpy aisles.
Under the maple, two women
trim the wilting green and even up
the stem bottoms. Each fistful now
market ready.

ii
I bend to gather stems, ridged, rough,
    then clip into the new growth
    rising from mounds of green.
I collect haloes of redolent wands, tips
    heavy with flower and early bees.
I hand my fistful, flowers down,
    to the next worker. She strips the leaves,
    fingering hard downward.
    She flips the bunch, hands it
to the next girl—one wrist atwist
    with rubber bands, and the other
gripped by a red clasp used to measure
    the girth of each bunch.
    Three times, she winds the soft band
    around the stems.
    The row is shorn of its diaphanous
    crown.
The perfume mixes now with then,
    drawing us into awakening.
Slacking off, we eat raspberries,
    still white downed,
    and eggs green-shelled,
    corn bread
    as big and flat as Kansas,
    and the butter soft.
We pull coffee from the urn
    pausing in such luxury,
    blessed so briefly
    inhaling slowly
    the scent of work.

SUSAN GRAY WILEY

Thanksgiving Cactus

Mother's cactus
profusion of grateful color
spreads its strength marks
into tender flesh.

Death gives them permanence
that life never cared to understand.

If only I knew as a child
to treat gently
those voices, those tears
boxing the fragrance
to use when needed.

Blood veins thicken with time
What is old becomes young
What is wrong becomes right
Connections, leap dubious knowing
to a clarity in the unknown.

Denial only fed the bonds
and strengthened

It feels warm
this acceptance of self
not as entity but assemblage
of those who loved
and were loved.

C. HUNTER DAVIS

Christmas Eve Dinner

Come evening, dinner was permitted.
Jellied fruits, sugared potatoes, rummed puddings,
buttered beans, salted hams, foods from another century
mounded in the dining room we seldom used.
A cloth filmed the table and
forks, gnarled with age and silver,
gifted from the ghost of an aunt, appeared.
So huge they stabbed our tonsils
and strained our wrists.

We seemed to chew off
the voluptuous plum designs
from plates willed
by still another cousin.
Yellowing and chipped
this china crated in a closet and
bruised our shins when reaching
for coats. They lay there like
the soft madness in our genes
that wreathed our lives so well:
my mother's ban on lighting
so only lamps drizzled light in our house ,
a brother's 2AM sleep walk
nearly twice a week ,
and my imagined whorl of characters
whose stories I manipulated
while trying to live my own.

In scarred glasses the water we never drank
would spill before grace was said.
It bled through the cloth and the table,
dripped down layers of aunts, cousins and old menus
to the floor where it lay
like a fine dusting of icing.

C. HUNTER DAVIS

A Cottonwood on My Birthday

Because I have decided to spend my birthday
under a cottonwood.
I lie in its generous shade
on this hot July day in the Wenas valley.
Somewhere between 20 and 40 years old,
pale and thin years that
crumble like tumbleweed
and wither below the stump.

Above an acorn woodpecker's knocks
compete with the western wood pewee's thrills
at a height the tree must have been
or maybe slightly smaller the year my mother
sat underneath shade with her Navy man
as they headed west, out of Texas
towards the watery Coast. She
could have sat down under this tree,
spread the remains of their picnic food.
and the cotton fluff of the *Populus salix*
covered her dress and her legs-
her beautiful "Overton Byrd legs"
that only certain relatives were genetically gifted.
"Are these western cotton?" and she gathered the fluff up in a scarf
and asked at the next filing station
where they did not have a coca cola .
"Cottonwood fluff, no good fer nothun'
but them trees is old and good fer yer firewood."
She let the fluff go by the Packard that
still had to make it over the mountains.

The tree was an adolescent
when my paternal grandfather left his sheep,
shook from his shoulders dust
that smelled of rattlesnakes.
And headed for the Coast.
He didn't want to die thirsty.
In the Great Plains, cottonwoods
were the tallest thing he'd ever seen.

And he configured mountains
out of the ones he saw on the grass lands.
He liked to think it was their honey fragrance
that led him across the Dakotas and Montana
until he reached the Wenas valley
50 miles short of the coast.
He took up a house in sight of the mountains
and went to cleaning offices , banks
and buildings.
He never did reach the Coast
I hear his sheep in the heart shaped
leaves that turn to ornaments in the wind
and thank him for his years of cleaning-
another gene I did not get.

The tree was trunk size when my great grandmother
began her journey west , pummeling herself
from the East with barely a clutch of people.
She used the cottonwoods
to cure rheumatism and take the cold out ,
brewed the bark so sweetly,
you could not taste the tannin.

She gave it to a son who went
bald at 7 after a fever,
and loved feathers, a gene
I did receive.
After so many infusions his hair grew in
wispy and the scalp always
scaly as the tree.
She died somewhere between
the ages I am today
near where my arms lay.
in the branches.

RON SIMONS

The firewood now burned
Bedstraw spreading, all spring green
Where the stack had been

ANN SPIERS

Mushroom

He promised
he would not go there
where everyone had gone before
off the road, through the mowed fields,
out into the space where the young
bend lower than autumn's sinking sun.

He said he didn't go there
after they all counted rain, drop by drop,
enduring school hours as chemistry
and botany folded into Thanksgiving break.

He said he was so sure he was not there
picking mushrooms, small beings of fast growth
among cow dung, the new wet, and stubble.
No, no one else was there
but when the sun gave up the sky,
he located the stars I had taught him
to sort into constellations.
And before he forgot he was there field side,
the stellar bits lost their holding pattern
and flew off , dozens of deserters, leaving him.
He wanted me to know
that snow geese honked into the dark.
He followed as the drift of ground fog
crawled across the wide field
and snagged on the far alders.

HELEN RUSSELL

bumpy road
to visit my old friend
our differences resurface

LYNDA SCHRAUFNAGEL

Comfort

Unlike the movies, people don't run after each other,
they let each other go: they're tired or bored, or they've had enough
    already,
like the night I was falling into that mood where, for no reason,
I imagined the world was watching and, ignoring it,
went to our longstanding dinner at Joan's, hoping it wouldn't hit
and I'd have to go, and not in an hour or fifteen minutes
but right away which, of course, is exactly what happened,
and it wasn't as if I didn't like Joan and her kid with his politically
    aware pals,
but when that moment came and, suddenly, nothing worked: not the
    music,
not someone offering a plate, I left and from the car
watched the people going back and forth on the porch,
smoking, chopping wood, and it all looked kind of mechanical but of
    course,
I was the one who was broken and everyone else, just doing what
    people do,
and when we got home and she was watching TV, I put on my coat,
    picked up my keys and left, and for a long time stood in the hallway
by the window, waiting for her to come, and it's really tiresome isn't it,
having to haul ourselves back in, like bringing in a stray that's
    forever in need of blessing.

JEAN AMELUXEN

The neighbor's dog
a surly cur
would shame another master

C. HUNTER DAVIS

Calling for Lillie

Although this March slings out a chill
and rain stains my face as I pause-
a woman in a summer shift, hemmed with
flowers drifts through her yard.

In a melody octaves higher
than my range, she calls for Lillie.
The song blooms beyond
our human imprint on the earth
and floats to the imperial sphere
of dogs.

In moments, if there still
are such things here,
Lillie should come:
paws prancing,
breath steamy from the outer reaches,
tail blurry with love
and then fur will
snow all over the woman's shift.

I hope Lillie will come
and come again
and the calling come and the come calling come
again and again
before I have to leave.

ROGER DAVIES

In Praise of the Pretend and the Rumpled

When the sergeant
was barking, the recruit's
mind was leaping
with the stray dog
across the field there,
as it sniffed its way
into an unknown destiny.
Where the boy's shirt
was meant to be flat
as a sheet of steel,
it was rumpled like
the ravine he imagined
the dog's nose mapped
in the memories of scent.
Clearly he wasn't A1 material;
Certainly he wouldn't do.
When the allegiance
to the Breakfast of Champions
was each one's destiny,
just like on TV,
he was seeing his family—
all leatherback turtles—
readying for the long
migration across
a white expanse of sea.

ROGER DAVIES

On The Occasion of the Bombing of Yugoslavia

Out my window I see
the Spruce are preparing
yet another assault
upon the Earth

The Spruces, getting ready
to shower down
life bombs

the little cruising missiles
armed and ready
with potent Spruce DNA

appearing this morning
after night maneuvers
~mysteries of the dark~

twig preparedness
launch of command
springing forth;

burst of life bombs
at the assigned moment
.. *Nova Scotia Spring*

smart bombs
looking for a receptive crater
under Robin reconnaissance

Spruce explosions,
the arsenal of Birth.

ROGER DAVIES

Wishful Thinking

Wish sounds like what happens
when the magician snaps the table cloth
away, off the table – *wish* – and all the plates,
knives, forks, spoons, and glasses remain,
as if friction momentarily flew out the
flung open window. Some people say
wishful thinking is air too thin to breathe,
but if you stop and think, one breath to the next,
wishfully
the wheels of your everyday world
the wheels of your trials
the wheels of your tribulations
the wheels of your love for the world
get a graceful dab of friction reducing grease.
If you listen just so, with your finest ear,
you'll hear how the abrasive scratch
diminishes, its incessant hark
waning, the oils soaking
in, the way hope does into thought.

JULI GOETZ MORSER

What if We Knew

We live our daily lives
Slicing through webs
With frantic speed
Ignorant
Of those gossamer lines
Connecting us

We believe
There is
Somewhere
To get to

When still
A single moment is all
We need
To feel

The full
Breathing
Breast
Of this our earth.

MARY G. L. SHACKELFORD

Surfeit

In these uncertain times
    it is enough
    to notice the sun moves north
    a little more each morning
    in my eastern window.

In this deep night
    it is enough
    to be shocked by the wide-eyed pupil of full moon
    swimming in an iris of Northern Light
    staring out of the darkness.

In this struggle and confusion
    it is enough
    that regular daily practice
    does accumulate in the knowing of my fingers
    though I will never match my mandolin teacher.

In these dying times
    it is enough
    to witness the purple spear of crocus
    push through the blanket of snow
    and hold its blossom in the bitter cold.

Even as earthquakes rock our cities
    and half the world starves
    from human greed
    Earth herself shows us every day
    to trust life.

It is enough.

ERIC HORSTING

Spring

This dead balloon stops me with its lavender
cord not trying to be the grass,
now green. The late April wind rustles
the cord's loops; the balloon wants to fly.
But the grass holds on, and the balloon
is burst, the black purple rubber
silent, split from a fragment
of itself a foot away, curled
like an egg. After ten minutes, I
notice a brown bit of dead
elm leaf, like an insect's wing.
The earth seeps quietly
up through my jeans.
The rain's damp anchors me.
Far off, I see a scarlet Frisbee
floating, hot, searching for someone's hands.

MARTA COU

pregnant, spring whispers
vermillion amaryllis
gingerly unfurls.

SHIRLEY FERRIS

Our Father of Red
Hear prayers of ripe tomatoes~
window sill rosary

JEAN CARPENTER

I Met April Today

As I drove through little white balls of hail on the way to Vashon Pharmacy
I reminded myself that it was just a little time ago I could not drive at all.
Now I bask in getting groceries and loving people waiting in line ahead of me instead of cursing them for their slow stupidity.
Cancer does that you know; it sorts out life's priorities sort of quickly.
Today I was sad about all the losses—house, job and general normalness.

Then I met April in Vashon Pharmacy.
In my usual boisterous manner I had bounded in the store advising "Y'all be careful out there…there's hail, though little it's he..ell."
As I waited to pick up the mountain of drugs that I need to survive this pretty red headed girl came up to me and said,
"Where you from?" I said "Where you from, Darlin'?"
Well goodness sakes alive, she was from South Carolina and lived in Columbia, Mississippi, just down the road a piece from my hometown.
We just bonded and talked like ole friends saying "we're fixing to do…" this and that.
"You know," she said, "talkin' Southern is just like talkin' lovin'."
We laughed and talked 'til a line formed behind us. Gracious Mandie, trying to serve, asked that we move around the corner.
Apologizing profusely to those waiting (good Southern girls do that you know), we moved around the corner to continue our talk.

As I was leaving and going to my car, my new friend April (what a touch of spring love that woman is) called out–"Jean, come see what I bought!"

I circled back under a gray now hail less sky, and looked as she brought out of the white pharmacy bag bright, colorful red, blue and yellow sun hats.

"They're for my nephews for Easter–aren't they just darlin'?"

"Absolutely,"' I cooed and then started weeping.

I told her of my great nephew Prescott who had died at 5 months old, only five months old, during my "brain find out" time; I never saw him.

April held me as I cried under the tree at Vashon Pharmacy.

It was later that night that I discovered with the pills I had paid for I had "shoplifted" BenGay to help neck and headaches.

Of course, being a good Southern girl I called and left a message of unintended theft. Actually, I don't need the salve because I met April today.

ROGER DAVIES

Preparing to Pretend to Knit at the Chemotherapy Clinic

I'll choose the long, elegant needles,
the ones appearing to be made of stainless.
For wool, homespun dyed with the juice
of roots and berries, giving the strands
the hues of November land and grey skies
and the remaining gorgeous leaves.
I could take out the soft skeins;
I could hold the needles
as my mother did—such nonchalant
competence; I could look out the window
to the fading Autumn day.

ERIC HORSTING

Heroism

Outside the shack, a large cedar tree with
branches trimmed to neat circular nodes,
regular wounds of death. The woodsman
has done his work.
He stands under the tree's shadow, Swedish saw
dangling orange and bullet-steel teeth quiet
in the early morning.

The dew drips from the woodsman's
graying beard as if it loves the scraggly curls
any mother would like to take sharpened razor
to. The woodsman shifts one booted foot slightly,
a sign of life, possibly, he'd rather not admit to.
It's been raining a long time in the Pacific
Northwest, and he's trying his best to notice the drops.

C. HUNTER DAVIS

The Bus Stop

The sun flirts with the earth ,
hellebores jaunt through the soil.
Snowdrops dimple faith in weak sun
and time is the verdict of the day,
as its defense we stand,
at the bus stop.
certain of destination,
the evidence of victory
One overgrown boy
with the looseness of 20 year olds
contests.
His fingers transparent
from the job and youth
Routines are respites from his life.
Opinions and coins drool from his pockets.
A black scarf refuses the spring
He is blatant with his strawed milk drink.

In that slack sound as he nears the cup end
I hear back 30 years
to a dishwasher motor
shoveling soap, and warmth and water
through the evening kitchen,
steam ghosting through its door.
The calibration clicks twice
for the water stream to funnel out,
a sound so precious in the vacant night,
so like the drain of his milk shake.
Before it ends Mrs. Nyman from next door
will turn on the melony light
in her own kitchen, so close to mine
we pass salt. She'll rub her eyes,

pull off her watch.
Her children emptied into bed,
her husband who falls nightly down a hole
to "Popular Mechanics" won't be heard
She'll think of nothing to remember,
read a recipe she'll never make,
or pluck at silver spoons in a jar.

Where are we?
Time must have not have won the case
even though there was so much testimony on its behalf—
a bus stop with quarters jingling
and sun on morning momentum
next to the black scarfed boy
and his paper cup,
spring still so fragile,
its' held in the arms of fir trees?

Or are we then
where a neighbor is in the pose of peace
and a washer's tones have
inoculated the day
with relief?

Time is just an affidavit
from light and bone

Light for the airiness of it,
the implausibility of time.
and bone like the sternum
that centers the brass buttons
on wool coats worn to shelter
the future.
.

CAL KINNEAR

A Peony

There I am laid out like a root. Eyes
shut, mouth shut.
Might as well be muck-earth.

Memory can get itself on fine
without me.
There'll always be some new poet

coming on. Sassy mouth, hot,
fire to burn down
a century.

I'll come back
a peony tall and silent
in August.

CAL KINNEAR

Dreamtime

Old sleep, old
nanny, old as rain, as rut, as red.
So old

you would expect her to be
rusty, gnarled, tough.
She is fresh

as new milk, loose
as combed hair.
Come along. It's nothing.

Float out on her limpid surface,
only faintly salt, in your slim
lapstrake dory,

just touching the oars now and then
with their long
graceful fingers,

the languid
eddies
they make.

ROGER DAVIES

Facebook Poem

Dear moon thank you
for choosing to be my friend

it is your face
in the book of my soul

that I choose always
to view

the beams you send
when old, when new

are always
a sliver of silver delight

I want you
to be in contact

whenever you rise
and I'll look to your face

smiling behind the pines
as you set

and even when
the power goes off
you're at your best

and so am I —
oh the silence of your face!
oh the silence of mine!

CATHERINE JOHNSON

On a Bright Summer Day

On a bright summer day
I stacked wood for the winter,
knowing how soon the rains would come,
the long gray wet hours, the chill and the wind.
I worked in a sleeveless shirt.
Sweat dripped from my brow
made streaks down my dirty face.
Half rounds and quarters,
I placed them, one against the other, glad
at fifty I can still bend and lift and carry,
small acts, I once took for granted.

Some year I will be forced by age and inevitable infirmity
to pay someone younger,
pay someone younger to do
what today, still comes easy.

This place we love,
with its steep roof and many windows,
with its high gutters and weathered wood
one day, it will become too much.

But for now we sand and stain,
climb ladders and fix hoses.
We pull weeds and spread chips,
take the door off its hinges, chisel out the rot and fill what we can
with brown sticky putty.
In the fading light we pick a gallon of blackberries,
tomorrow we'll make sweet jam.
We are doing what people have done for centuries –
in the blaze of summer, we make way for winter.

ROGER DAVIES

The Argentinean Blueberries

The Argentinean Blueberries
travel the well-worn forced migration route
to Nova Scotia. Their northern cousins
have left the bush—what remains
of them now frozen to the ground,
but most likely eaten, in late summer,
by bears birds humans.
The birds have migrated,
chirping singing eating
in their southern bush.
The bears sleep.

MARTA COU

Cuba of My Heart

Palm fronds sway languidly;
Curved trunks,
Bent but not flawed,
Protrude effortlessly from sugar sands
That gently slope
Towards a shimmering turquoise shore.

I visit there often—sometimes every day,
And perpetuate
A memory
I cannot ever forget.

When I think of home—my real home,
The place I came from,
The place I left,
I feed the fire that keeps it going;
Then I am warmed from skin-to- marrow
And back again.

My deep affection has never waned,
I hear and smell and feel and see it.
Sometimes,
Eyes closed,
I stick out my tongue
To taste the saline, moist, caressing Caribbean breeze.

Should the choice not be mine?
I will wait another 40 years,
And even then,
If only as mere particles of dust,
I will return.

Ashen specs of my scorched heart—that dust,
Indistinguishable from the sugar sand,
Will fill the crevices left there for me
By a past I have kept alive.

Content to be home,
I will rest there,
Safely anchored,
Settling in beneath the shelter of the swaying palm fronds,
Never to fly away on another heart-breaking departure.

ERIC HORSTING

Mortality

In the early morning, Lake Geneva
can't shed its shroud. Drying in Vaud seems
remote now that you've left it. Halted
by the water, you've pulled off the road to stare
at the flat tire. The air is crumbling,
wanting to rain. Your glasses weep with mist.
The wheel won't rise by itself, and your back
stiffens as you reach for the tire iron.
The water behind you sizzles softly.
You turn to see the dock, the small ramp,
the mail boat, or so you think, sliding
into place. Its white gleams, and the blue
and red trim is perfect. It sits still.
It rocks gently on its own waves. No others
disturb the lake's flat skin. Soon the only
sound is the smooth engine, whirring out of gear.
The boat is waiting. So are you. No one arrives.
Ghosts are at the wheel, delirious.

INA WHITLOCK

Will the Time Come?

Will the time come, when
no carpet of green covers the lawn
in yellow buttons of spring?
When the planets' plants fail
under mismanagement, and the earth
turns rubble-up in asphalt and debris?
Will I regret the loss of my dislike –
dead-heading patrols, and the sight
of miniscule silvery wings,
progeny, escaping by paraglide,
generation after generation,
and though I think that other wees
could satisfy the hunger of the bees,
will I, regret, when sunlit paths
of dandelions disappear?

ERIC HORSTING

Coal Miners and Other People

To someone who can see
through earth, we
are carving a deadly
shape, like a tree
with branches of air
thin enough to crawl through,
thick enough to keep us down.

After twenty or thirty years
the tree begins to feel like
home. We come
to love its form
so much we have
to breathe it in.

Soon, our lungs blossom,
go to dark seed, breed
black twigs and fruit
slippery with red drops.

Like the dream of all romantics,
we are becoming one
with nature, and there is nothing
we can do about it.

JANICE RANDALL

Home

A mythical place discovered in a dream
Journey from dark narrow passages where danger lurks
massive boulders barbed wire steep climb
insurmountable, impossible
Bleeding hands and torn feet miraculously arrive
Beyond the mountaintop
They welcome me, young and old
radiant, ten strong they seek an even dozen
Travel with us, come along for the ride
They whisper Valhalla, a beautiful language I can't comprehend
Yet somehow understand
But I'm just trying to get home
Can you take me there?
Valhalla via Kansas and back again
A place for heroes and warriors
Life's battleground
Golden reverie
Not home yet.

INA WHITLOCK

High Tide

Bulkhead, barrier against high tide
   of days, years, anniversaries
      moon's pull, storm's rage,
         seawall that keeps you far.

Sea gulls, a pair, hunker,
   then cry on wing retrieving
      from stone-cracked shells
         succulence, and I dream;

Undertow of memories and molecules
   night's dark liquidity,
      an iridescent flow of starfish,
      mollusks, sea kelp's sway,

Sea horses, white cresting manes
   plunging deep, and the briny kiss
      of wavelets on shores of skin,
         rounding bays, inlets, high tide.

ROGER DAVIES

Earth Hour

After we've turned off
the TV and the lights,
and all the instant-ons,
with their little red glowing coals,
we'll go next to the bullet machines,
pulling the plug
on each and everyone of them,
stopping the endless flow of slugs,
and then moving on
to the nuclear hair-triggers,
selecting OFF for sanity,
the screens going to black—
so we can all breathe into the silence a sigh of relief—
so we can close the staring paranoid eyes of the radars—
and simply stop, and look to one another with
opening eyes.

C. HUNTER DAVIS

Apples Fall

The apple tree in the vacant lot insults its namesake.
Although it approaches harvest like every-
other. Its sour and scabby adolescent
fruits hang by threads.
Green and misshapen from neglect,
they're are ready for the Fall
immediately to liver spotted waste,
the senile muck of storm drains.

It's in the falling, the feared Fall
where they have a chance.
If only it could last –
that time between
the attachment to unfit limbs
and decay
-long enough to steal food and then realize
you could become a farmer and provide food,
-long enough to flunk out of school
and return as an architect,
-long enough for the life in the open air
to heal the rash of despair
and the bruise of anger.

SUSAN GRAY WILEY

Through the Looking Glass

"Happy September 11th
utters Alice
jumping out of a New York hole.
"Retaliation still needed"
echoes the March Hare
casting dark shadows
upon Mad Hatter's Tea Party
"Off with their heads"
yells the Queen of Hearts
swinging necks of obedient men.

Another sun rises
still hot from summer
knows nothing, cares not
simply dries blood
scabs over
leaves the scar.

What will it take
to erase the blight
make skin smooth
use shadows for tag

"Fill the hole with magic beans"
yells Alice
The Cheshire Cat smiles
Thinking of possibilities.

ERIC HORSTING

Holland: Hongerwinter, 1944-45 (The War Years End)

A boy sits on the kitchen floor, watching
it disappear. Soon the boards won't hold
the stove that burns them, and the frying
pan will fall with its burden of sautéed
tulip bulbs as far as the ground that grew
them. The man who sits outside waits for the snow
to melt; his pants won't let go the ice beneath.
He stares at the sky; it's gray, as ever.
He waves his arms like a windmill, but the air
pretends he's lost. He is. In Rotterdam,
my aunt slices her wrists, again. It's
getting to be the way she lives, live on.

LONNY KANEKO

Coming Home from Camp
Her words to no one:1946

It seems like the same thing all over again.
But worse. One room. Three of us in one bed,
a hot plate, sink, no refrigerator. The milk
spoils on the window sill. The bathroom's public.
I scour the tub twice. And no job.
Daddy can't find a job. He's tried.
The twenty-five they gave us as we left the gate's
not enough for rent, food, and tools.
I've tried the P.T.A. The teachers try
to be conversational. The other parents smile
and look away.

                                    The farmers in Idaho
were shocked that we spoke English just like them.
They thought we'd be killers, spies who spoke
strange words and bowed a lot. We fixed
our smiles at them when they asked,
"Why have they sent you here?"
Heck, we had just as much right to be happy.
I tried to make the barrack a home and ignore
the racket the coyotes made at night.
You should have heard them. And the thunder.

In this hotel, I look out the window and see
only a brick wall four feet away.
No sky. I guess Camp wasn't so bad. At least
we had a yard, even if the fence was there
to keep us in. The men folks learned to make
tables and chairs, and toys like Mickey Mouse
and Pluto. I learned to embroider flowers and birds
on a branch.

　　　　Here there's the whine of cars and howls
from trains grinding into the station night
after night. There's no reason to say,
"Things will get better." Daddy's got to try harder.
But he won't. Or can't. I never knew
this side of him. After a while you realize
that nothing changes. You don't say, "Keep trying."
You know that nothing changes. It just repeats.
And then you stop. You don't know when it happens.
　　　　But it does.

ERIC HORSTING

1945: Oma In Amsterdam As The War Ends

You are still alive. You brush the canvas
with pink-red brick until a vision of a wall
builds its peculiar light solidity:
a diagonal slash of shadow splits
the painting in half: a late afternoon orange
splashes the stones above, where a slice
of Dutch azure peeks; and below, like Bruegel,
you hide, in a corner, what you most admire,
blossoms you'll pick one day to paint, alone,
in a vase in your studio, which stands, still.

ERIC HORSTING

Manifesto

For some of us, there appear to be choices;
there is time enough to assume the voices

we appreciate or lust after, the masks
a fey and sophisticated city asks

us to slip on when it wishes, when we will.
Such moments are fraught with elegance, a chill

and serene loveliness weathered like the arch
at Washington Square, like the consistent march

of jackboot soldiers across Europe's brick squares,
who think new uniforms will fend off the glares

of sullen peasants who've seen all the changes
and know the ruddy boys' bodies, the ranges

and ends of their lives, like theirs, full of sadness
near the end, at the start ordained with the kiss

of belief, with the ordinary advice
that, if this doesn't work, then something else might.

ROGER DAVIES

Fifties

Women are learning
to be pals
with machines

White men
with fresh haircuts,
the ones who came back,
stare silently down
at home improvements.
Nightmares will soon be flattened
by the new home screens:
McCarthy prepares his face.
People put away socks
and head out to the big screen
to see Day, Hope, Reagan.

We are in the moments
between fission and fusion.
Electricity with flow without measure
to a wealth of motors.
There will be push buttons
for every deserving hand.
A woman shows another
how satisfying it is
to put butter in a freezer.

The smooth road
of the 50's
is opening up before us:
It is the time of deserving.

INA WHITLOCK

Quartet on a Theme of Shostakovich

From where – Dresden – this deep brooding
   strike on cities of my mind, music
      thrust by the bow across the ribs,
     spirals of hurt sounding

through chambers of my heart, the strings
   gut searing resonance, in dark recess
     where utmost sorrow springs,
       loosened from decades, centuries,

cloistered chains of minds – beyond all music –
   that inflict not sweetly, nor from glory
     but the gall of human failing—
      a dissonance the quartet plays,

yet sustains, in such tenderness
   the sacred sounds of suffering,
     humankind's music for remembering—
      the ultimate, enduring tone.

INA WHITLOCK

Unless

Unless I live as you
I will never know
what strife you feel,
the anger of life,
rock-thrower, bloodied soul,
precious mother's child—
caught on emotion's dark wave
of hate, no amnesty
from bullets, sticks, stones, tears,
tear gas made in the U.S.A.,
carnage on streets of Cairo,
or anywhere, in midst of a mob,
the sacrifices of self
exchanged for a dream of freedom,
a bargain with adversity—

yet, I must be your witness
with my eyes, heart, and voice.

MARY G. L. SHACKELFORD

Fall Poem - October 11, 2001

I.
In the cacophony
of fall garden exploding with
the last gasps of thrown seeds and
crickets hidden in the brittle grass,
I celebrate the long labor of
summer. Quick fall
days spin out. I stand in
the high circle of stone
to pluck the stories of
constellations from the night.
The Summer Triangle —
Vega in Lyra, Deneb
in Cygnus, and
Altair in Aquila
give way to the Great Square of Pegasus
as Orion rises now
to chase the Bull
and the Pleiades towards
the dark of winter.

II.
Just one month since
the last gasps of
so many, hurled
willfully and unknowing
into sudden terror and
unholy violent end
seared into the eyeballs of
every one of us. Alive
in the dread carried in bellies
that shrink from what's to come:

a long, hard winter
for mothers and children
picking through the rubble.

We hide our children and send
dollars and prayers against
starvation in the killing fields
of Afghanistan.
Our imagination rises
unbidden and inevitable,
from the smoking mass grave
in Manhattan and
the parentless children left
to spend lifetimes seeking
information about hate
and terror and freedom
fighters in *jihad*; flags waving
America the Beautiful,
to ride the breath
of daily *tonglen*
through the shortening days
into what is known
in the visceral gut of all women
who love men and bear
children and bake bread
of daily life in a place
bombed and strafed
twice in twenty years and
regularly ravaged by
random cruelty in
long lifetimes of
centuries-old oppression.

We know there is
the terrible hopelessness of
despair. And I know,
riding the breath of god
into the belly of
an Afghan woman,
that she struggles to
greet another morning
with the children.

III.
Boxes and boxes of apples waiting
for the press, and, on the table,
lines of jars with the red
thickness of tomato juice, the
translucent hue of grape juice
we have put aside for
the taste of summer sun when
we drink on emerging, birthing
from winter sweat lodges. The incredible,
delicate blush on yellow pears;
two rosebuds defy the crisp
mornings to open gently in the warming
sun of high fall noon.

ROGER DAVIES

Prayer in the Form of Cranes
Prayer for the Future, spoken into the Dreamtime

The paper cranes
flutter down
into the future,
extending their legs
to touch the Earth.

Yet first they fly back,
through time
from the vast skies
of prayer.

Their careful fold lines
are being spirited
into sinew
and into
the living bones of flight.

Their bright
and hopeful surfaces
evoke themselves
into feathers,
seeking life in air.

It is the moment
of a thousand muscled
wings moving.

A thousand times a thousand
white Cranes step into
dawn.

They are flying now,
rising high in the heat
over the the unfused
sands of Almagordo

They are circling
the Quonset huts
of Los Alamos
and the prophecies
of the ancients.

They are heading
toward the internment
compounds of the American
dispossessed.

They are flying
up the Potomac.

They are coming
to the Atolls of the Pacific
and the tarmacs
and the bombsights
that can see no child

They have reached
the wingtips
of the Enola Gay.
The Cranes reach out
to one another in spirit language.

Now they are about to fly
under death's metallic imagination.

They are raising evil
out of its own way.
The altimeters
and the pilots
and the crazed generals
have lost their voices
to the songs of birds.

The Cranes
are lifting
the U.S. Air force
to a thousand Crane sky.

Over Hiroshima
the one and only sun
rises.

The waters
of the Motoyasu River
flow gently
by the domed building.

The smallest children
lift their clear and shining eyes
and their small faces
to the Cranes
Amen
It is a day
for Crane observing
Amen
It is a day
to move the ten fingers
of your perfect two hands

Amen
It is a day
to make careful folds
from kind memories
Amen
It is a day
to learn the patterns
of peace
Amen
It is a day to reach out
to the children of the future,
saying "Not one of you will be
born to the slow death
of radiation"
Amen
It is a day
when Peace will be born
in the shape of a Crane
Amen

INA WHITLOCK

60 Seconds

Were this my last moment to tell you, my darlings,
ways of being in this world, what could I say
that might remain of a lifetime
so clearly not your own?

Yours, new hemispheres, neurons translate
in the brain, in the pulse of your time,
screens of mind informed, life lived
in joy, pain, birth, death.

We call destiny – destination for tasks
endeavors, artifacts – contrivances
that fail and fall, society
amok in gore.

Beauty in nature, the only absolute – fleeting
is saved by sentience of life
lived aware that all
future now.

A last moment holds nothing to bequeath
of the plethora of being, but hope
that love
remains.

INA WHITLOCK

Croak On

Croak on, old frog,
   the white butterfly
      flutters away.

Sounds of
   your comic song
      end summer's day

Soften earth's burnt edge
   where roots and timbers die
      and leaves not gathered

Rot in fetid pools,
   harboring no seasons
      or solace to survive

Unless we waken
   to millennial songs—
      so croak on, old frog

Conjure the birds
   from silences;
      a prince to kiss

The white butterfly
   of truth and beauty,
      so fragile, so fleeting.

Croak on, old frog,
   reveal the folly of
      forgetful men.

ROGER DAVIES

when the last cell phone
is silent—

sound of crickets

HELEN RUSSELL

old moon-viewing friend
how does it look
from heaven

HELEN RUSSELL*

first night in new digs
arranging furniture
I no longer have.

* This is Helen's final haiku, dictated to the hospital nurse on the evening of Helen's death, January 10, 2011 at age 101.

MICHAEL FEINSTEIN

hope, the space
between the kingfisher
and the new moon

AUGUST (GUS) HOLMES*

Everyone is laughing
All day the sun shines
Rafts ride down the stream
Tall trees tower
Here we are.

*written at age 6, when Gus went with his class to Fern Cove for the whole school day.

CONTRIBUTORS

JEAN AMELUXEN
Jean and Fritz Ameluxen still live in the Vashon home where they raised their children. Jean is retired after a long career with State Government in Olympia. She has finished her second book; a novel set on the Island during World War II; and takes great pleasure from the poetry and fellowship of the Vashon Haiku Group.

JILL BRADENFELS ANDREWS
Jill Brandenfels Andrews lives on Vashon Island with husband, Murray, and corgi, Rufus. She earned her Ph.D while a principal in the Bellevue schools, and later worked for the Gates Foundation schools grant and the Institute for Educational Inquiry. Jill and Murray have traveled widely, and are always happy to come home to enjoy the beach and host members of their combined family: 7 children, 18 grandchildren, 1 great grandchild.

PAUL BACKSTROM
Paul Backstrom lives in Kirkland, Washington, with his wife and college-age son. After getting degrees in English, he switched to writing computer language, but still finds in poetry the best way to distill, resolve, and remember human experience. These poems were previously published by King County Metro/4Culture Poetry on Buses.

DOROTHY HALL BAUER
I was working on my little books, "Islanders, Meet Your Neighbors" when Edeen Parrish invited me to come to the poetry group. The monthly meeting with those seasoned and talented poets in Ina Whitlock's living room was like the push from behind that I got thirty years ago from meetings with Joyce Delbridge and the Night Writers at the Blue Heron. Joyce said, "just tell us your story" and memories came out of the deep that I thought could never be dug up. I couldn't stop writing. The five or six poets in Ina's living room didn't suggest. They

just offered up their poems and soon I was offering mine up too for all to see.

KAJIRA WYN BERRY
Kaj Wyn Berry delights in being alive *every* day, but some days are even better when a haiku comes along. All sorts of other information on my website: kajirawynberry.com.

JEAN CARPENTER
Jean Carpenter wrote her first book, *The Vashon Years: Portraits of the Spirit*, while recovering from a bout of brain cancer. She and her husband Scott retired to Vashon from Bellevue, WA where Jean had been a "politico" and "justice maker." Her new work in progress, *Almost White Trash*, chronicles her early years in Mississippi as an integrationist in the land of segregation.

MARTA COU
Marta Cou is an artist, writer, and passionate supporter of arts in schools, healthcare, and political freedom. Originally from Cuba and exiled in 1960 at age seven during the exodus of Cuban children to other countries, Marta draws from her cherished indelible experiences; her life and art are infused with gratitude for the cultures and beauty she has witnessed. Having also lived in Jamaica, Puerto Rico, Hawaii, and now Vashon, Marta is an inveterate "island girl".

ROGER DAVIES
I'm the brother of Jeanie Okimoto, editor and publisher of *The Weird World Rolls On*. For years I have shared poems with her, and she has always let me know how much she has liked them. For the most part that is what I have done with poems—shared them with friends and family. Poems are a way of voicing my way of being in the world.

    I live in Halifax, Nova Scotia, Canada, where I am an active Quaker, grandparent, photographer, peace and environmental activist, and partner of my best friend Helen.

C. HUNTER DAVIS
(Caroline) Hunter Davis was born with rainy Pacific Northwest blood into a family that loves stories. She lives in an old schoolhouse underneath fir and fruit trees with collections of her words, her family and animals on Vashon Island in Puget Sound.

MICHAEL FEINSTEIN
Michael Feinstein is a writer who lives on Vashon Island.

SHIRLEY FERRIS
After 40 years of teaching/counseling, I appreciate more time to travel, create, explore the outdoors, and enjoy family and friends. For me haiku opens a door to thankfulness. Island living beckons me to wonder and nurtures my spirit. It is an honor to be included with fellow poets in a book that supports VCC, where both my parents completed their life journeys in loving care.

MARGARET HELDRING
Margaret Heldring lives and works in Seattle, Washington and nearby Vashon Island. She is a clinical psychologist and teacher in family medicine. She spent eleven years in Washington, D.C. working in the U.S. Senate and other venues for public policy. As she approaches full-time retirement, she enjoys time with her grandchildren, pottery, walking, and writing.

AUGUST (GUS) HOLMES
My family lives on a farm with sheep, chickens, dogs, cats, an orchard and a big vegetable garden. We are almost always outdoors. I like to bike, play soccer and baseball and read early in the morning.

ERIC HORSTING
Eric Horsting has published more than 100 poems in such journals as *Agni*, *Denver Quarterly*, *Literary Review*, *Poetry East*, and *Poetry West*, and he was for five years poetry editor of *The Antioch Review*. He taught poetry writing courses at all levels for 32 years at Antioch College in

Yellow Springs, Ohio. He is currently teaching an on-going workshop in creative writing sponsored by Vashon Allied Arts at the Blue Heron.

CATHERINE JOHNSON
After seventeen years of teaching graduate education, Catherine now devotes her time to farming, writing and craniosacral therapy. Her essays have appeared in the following anthologies: *Face to Face*, *Teaching with Fire* and *The Nature of an Island*. She lives with her partner on Vashon Island where she is working on a memoir and raising chickens.

KATE JOHNSON
Kate Johnson currently resides in California, where she splits her time (less evenly than she'd like) between Silicon Valley and the High Sierra. While driving back and forth with her boyfriend, Dan, and their imaginary dog, she enjoys reading Steinbeck, Fine Cooking, Trail Runner, Backpacker Magazine, and her favorite proof of the quadratic formula. She also enjoys concocting schemes to embarrass her beloved dad, to whom her poem is dedicated.

LONNY KANEKO
Lonny Kaneko's new poems in this anthology were drawn from poetry correspondences with poet Sharon Hashimoto; over the past decade each poet emailed a poem a day for a month. Lonny has also written plays with friend Amy Sanbo and has fiction in *The Big Aiiieee* and *Asian American Literature*. His chapbook is *Coming Home from Camp*. He also received a National Endowment for the Arts fellowship. He teaches English at Highline College.

CAL KINNEAR
Vashon Island poet Cal Kinnear, now retired, has been teacher, bookseller, modern dancer, waiter, carpenter, non-profit fundraiser and administrator. His poems have been published locally in *Crab Creek Review*, *Point No Point*, *Pontoon* and *Fine Madness*; he won *Fine Madness'* 2003 Nelson Bentley prize. *A Walk in Bardo* was published in 2008 by Blue Begonia Press. Raven Chronicles published a suite of his poems,

Heart Range, online (http://ravenchronicles.org/Nature/heartrange-cover.htm), in November of 2009.

JULI GOETZ MORSER
Juli Goetz Morser loves words and thanks her parents for cultivating her passion for them. Juli writes feature articles for newspapers and magazines, copy for online companies and blogs for nonprofits, has written documentaries and travel videos, and organized author readings for her community. But mostly Juli delights when her poetry muse calls out. Juli lives on Vashon Island with her husband and daughter and likes watching her dog watch the eagles fly by.

EDEEN MARLOWE PARISH
Edeen Marlowe Parish is a retired high school librarian, and community college teacher who has a love of geology, poetry and especially her family. Originally from Tennessee, she lived for many years in California. She and her husband live on Vashon Island.

JANICE RANDALL
Writer of stories, poetry and random phrases since age 8, Janice loves to access the hidden recesses of imagination and sleeping subconscious of the dreamworld to help make sense of life's every-day preposterous ambiguities. She is ever grateful for friendship and family, good health and the sweet daily comforts of her Island home in the woods.

HELEN RUSSELL
In 1998, Helen Russell started the Vashon Island's haiku gathering, Mondays at Three, at Paradise Cove, in her beach cabin. Still meeting monthly, her haiku-sharing group now numbers a dozen members. She graduated from the University of Washington in 1930 (she played shortstop for the UW women's baseball). Her prize-winning haiku are published in many journals and anthologies. She wrote the haiku in this book in her last years. She died in 2011, her 101st year of life.

LYNDA SCHRAUFNAGEL

A friend of the editor of this collection, Lynda Schraufnagel lived on Vashon Island in the mid-1980's. Originally from Wisconsin, she died of cancer a short time after her fortieth birthday on January 4, 1991. Lynda was awarded a 1989-90 Writing Fellow at the Fine Arts Center in Provincetown, Massachusetts. Her poem "Carnival" was published in *Feminist Studies*, 1987; "Trappings" was selected for *Best American Poetry, 1989*, after first appearing in *Shenandoah*; and "Trial" was published in the *Western Humanities Review* and was then selected for *The Best American Poetry, 1992*.

MARY G. L. SHACKELFORD

Mary G. L. Shackelford has been writing for all sorts of venues and making books on Vashon Island since the days of Laughing Dog Press, a women's collective active in the 1980's. She is grateful for this opportunity to share her work.

RON SIMONS

Ron Simons is a retired professor of psychiatry and anthropology who has worked extensively in SE Asia. He first learned of haiku, then a foreign and relatively unknown poetic form, in the mid-fifties from Gilbert Highet's renowned radio program "People, Places, and Books." He has been writing them since. Ron is an instructor (Junkakan) in the Ikenobo school of Japanese flower arranging and lives on Vashon with his wife, tile artist, Mary Lynn Buss and his standard poodle, Lily.

ANN SPIERS

Ann Spiers is the 2011-12 Vashon Poet Laureate. For the Vashon Poetry Fest 2011, she curated a gallery show called *Broadsides: Poems on Paper*, featuring more than 40 Northwest poetry broadsides, work including calligraphy, letter press, and new media. She is keeper of Vashon's Poetry Post in the Village Green where folks post and read poems. Her recent poetry chapbooks are *What the Rain Does* (Egress Studio Press) and *A Wild Taste* (May Day Press).

INA WHITLOCK

I came to poetry through art and writing. I have published *Eating the Chinese Pear* and *Sketches from Paraguaná, Venezuela*. Another book is in production—*Bree*, stories written half a century ago about growing up in the Midwest. I was born and raised in Nebraska, lived overseas many years, and now work from my Vashon Island home. After the death of my husband, I published *Of Love and Loss*, a small book of poems.

SUSAN GRAY WILEY

Teacher, dramatist, hiker, biker, gardener, traveler, and dreamer. Sue has lived with her husband on Vashon Island the past 42 years in a Century old farmhouse raising 3 kids, chickens, dogs, cats, and horses. She remembers writing children stories for childhood basement productions then on to teach creative writing in elementary schools and directing plays. Her current love is playing with 6 grandkids on a treasure hunt through Vashon fields.

www.ingramcontent.com/pod-product-compliance
Lightning Source LLC
Chambersburg PA
CBHW031257110426
42743CB00040B/695